PATTERNS IN FASHION
DESSINS DANS LA MODE
MUSTER IN DER MODE

MACARENA SAN MARTÍN

PATTERNS IN FASHION

DESSINS DANS LA MODE
MUSTER IN DER MODE

EVERGREEN

© 2009 EVERGREEN GmbH, Köln

Publisher: Paco Asensio

Editorial coordination: Anja Llorella Oriol

Editor and texts: Macarena San Martín

English translation: Tabitha Michaels

French translation: Anthony Rousseau

German translation: Ursula Seibert

English proof-reading: Carla Parra Escartín

French proof-reading: Céline Brandy

German proof-reading: Sabine Holz

Art director: Emma Termes Parera

Graphic design and layout: Raquel Marín Álvarez

Printed in Spain

ISBN 978-3-8365-1169-8

FROM THE DRAWING BOARD TO THE SHOP WINDOW

Since the big retail stores stormed onto the market just a little over a decade ago, the world of fashion has become a more affordable place for most of us, and one of the consequences of this is that we now tend to replace the garments in our closets much more often than before. As a result, each new collection now comprises a larger number of garments, giving fashion designers more scope when producing new creations. Moreover, fashion illustration has regained its popularity in recent years and is now, once more, considered a design discipline and has varying styles, and a growing number of devotees and renowned exponents. Bearing in mind these two tendencies, it is hoped that fashion designers—whether they themselves are experienced in drawing or they work in collaboration with illustrators or graphic artists—want to incorporate works of art into their designs in order to elaborate unique, innovative creations. Garments have become a new medium for graphic artists to exhibit their work, giving them easier access to the general public.

Our eyes have therefore gradually become accustomed to seeing different motifs in shop windows and they have become an all-encompassing phenomenon from which no garment can escape, be it daywear, evening wear, summer fashion, winter fashion, footwear or headgear. We can now find evening dresses, tracksuits, raincoats, swimwear, hats and sneakers stamped over and over again with features that brighten them up and set them apart from the rest.

As these infinitely repeated graphic elements—called patterns—are the best type of artwork to elaborate full prints (100 percent patterned fabrics), they are usually symmetrical, making fabrics appear as if they have no beginning and no end, no right way up and no wrong way around. This enables the various pieces of a garment to be cut in different directions, meaning that fabric can be used optimally and that the different directions are undetectable once the garment is sewn. In addition to symmetry, when designing patterns, other variables are also taken into account: one of the most important of these is that the pattern will be printed onto a fabric that will be used to create a fashion garment or accessory. This means that the body's curves and forms breathe motion into the designs, lending them qualities that they did not have when laid out on the cutting table.

The patterns in this compilation are both original and innovative; they also boast a wide range of motifs, be they tables jockeying for position on a T-shirt, an iceberg that climbs up the hem of trousers or hammers and wrenches that dance across a dress. Yet, some things never change: stripes, polka dots, paisley and animal prints are timeless. And for this reason we have included them in this selection, such as designs that catch our attention because they play with color, proportion or techniques to reinvent these classics and give them a new twist.

D'UNE ESQUISSE À LA VITRINE

Depuis l'apparition massive des magasins de grande distribution il y a un peu plus de dix ans, le monde de la mode est devenu accessible à une grande majorité de personnes et, par conséquent, la rotation des vêtements dans les armoires est beaucoup plus importante qu'autrefois. Cela se traduit par une augmentation de la production de vêtements pour chaque collection, d'où la possibilité accrue pour les créateurs de jouer avec de nouveaux modèles. D'autre part, ces dernières années, l'illustration est redevenue une discipline artistique avec des styles variés qui comptent de plus en plus d'adeptes et de représentants de renom. En tenant compte de ces deux variables, il faut s'attendre à ce que les créateurs de mode désirent, afin d'obtenir des résultats uniques et innovateurs, intégrer des illustrations à leur design, soit en les utilisant eux-mêmes au cours de leur réalisation, soit en travaillant en collaboration avec des illustrateurs ou des artistes graphiques. Pour ces derniers, les vêtements deviennent de plus un nouveau support d'exposition, qui leur permet d'exhiber leur travail et, par conséquent, toucher plus facilement le public.

C'est ainsi que peu à peu nos yeux se sont habitués à voir différents motifs dans les vitrines, jusqu'à ce que cela devienne une fièvre qui n'épargne rien : ni le jour ni la nuit, ni l'hiver ni l'été, ni les pieds ni la tête. On trouve de la même façon des robes de soirée et des survêtements, des coupe-vent et des maillots de bain, des casquettes et des baskets, couverts d'éléments qui se répètent encore et encore sur toute la surface, en l'égayant et en la faisant ressortir par rapport au reste.

VOM ENTWURF INS SCHAUFENSTER

Ces éléments graphiques qui se répètent à l'infini sont des motifs et c'est le type d'illustration le mieux adapté pour réaliser des *full prints* (des toiles entièrement imprimées) puisqu'ils sont symétriques et donnent l'impression visuelle que la toile n'a ni début ni fin, ni endroit ni envers. De cette manière, les différentes pièces qui composent un vêtement peuvent être coupées dans plusieurs sens, afin de tirer le meilleur parti de la toile, et, au moment de la coudre, on ne remarquera pas les différents sens. Au moment de concevoir les motifs, d'autres variables à prendre en compte viennent s'ajouter à la symétrie : l'une des plus importantes c'est le fait que le motif sera imprimé sur une toile avec laquelle on confectionnera un vêtement ou un accessoire de mode. Cela signifie que les courbes et les volumes du corps donneront de la dynamique aux designs et leur conféreront des valeurs qu'ils n'avaient pas à plat.

Les thématiques des motifs présentés ici sont originales et innovantes. On peut y trouver des tables qui couvrent chaotiquement un tee-shirt, ou bien un iceberg qui monte le long de l'ourlet d'un pantalon, ou encore des marteaux et des clés anglaises qui batifolent sur toute la surface d'une robe. Cependant, nous savons qu'il y a des éléments immuables et c'est pour cela qu'ils font partie de cette sélection : il y aura toujours les rayures, les points, le paisley et les motifs animaliers. Les designs de ce type qui ont attiré notre attention sont ceux qui détournent l'idée et créent de nouvelles versions de ces classiques, que ce soit en termes de combinaisons de couleurs, de la proportion des éléments ou de la technique employée.

Mit dem massiven Einzug der großen Handelsketten auf den Modemarkt vor etwas mehr als einem Jahrzehnt wurde Mode auch für die breite Masse erschwinglich. Dies hatte zur Folge, dass sich der Umschlag an Kleidungsstücken in den Schränken bedeutend erhöhte. Gleichzeitig stieg auch die Produktion der Kleidungsstücke aller Kollektionen, und damit boten sich Designern größere Chancen, mit neuen Modellen zu spielen. Andererseits machte auch die Illustration in den letzten Jahren vermehrt auf sich aufmerksam und hat sich zu einer Kunstdisziplin mit verschiedenen Stilrichtungen entwickelt, die immer mehr Anhänger findet und berühmte Vertreter hervorbringt. Angesichts dieser beiden Faktoren war zu erwarten, dass Modedesigner auf der Suche nach einzigartigen und innovativen Entwürfen auch Illustrationen aufgreifen – indem sie für ihre Dessins selbst damit experimentieren oder aber die Zusammenarbeit mit Illustratoren und Grafikern suchen. Diese nutzen Kleidungsstücke als Trägermaterial und als neuartiges Präsentationsmittel, mit dem sie das Publikum leichter erreichen können.

Dieser Entwicklung haben wir es zu verdanken, dass sich die Schaufenster nach und nach mit immer vielfältigeren Mustern gefüllt haben. Das Gestaltungsfieber lässt nichts unberührt, weder Alltags- noch Abendkleidung, weder Winter- noch Sommerkollektionen, weder Fußbekleidung noch Kopfbedeckung. Abendkleider und Jogginganzüge, Regenmäntel und Bademoden, Mützen und Sneakers … allesamt sind sie mit Designelementen bedeckt, die im beständigen Rapport Flächen beleben und Kleidungsstücke einzigartig machen.

Muster mit derlei grafischen Elementen, die sich unendlich oft wiederholen, eignen sich am besten für die Herstellung von *full prints* (komplett bedruckte Stoffe), weil sie im Allgemeinen symmetrisch sind. Dies bedeutet, dass der Stoff optisch weder Anfang noch Ende, weder eine linke noch eine rechte Seite aufweist, sodass die einzelnen Teile eines Kleidungsstücks in verschiedene Richtungen geschnitten werden können. Auch der Stoff selbst lässt sich optimal nutzen, weil beim Nähen die verschiedenen Richtungen nicht festzustellen sind. Neben der Symmetrie gelten für einen solchen Musterentwurf aber noch weitere Faktoren, etwa die Tatsache, dass mit dem bedruckten Stoff ein Kleidungsstück oder Modeaccessoire hergestellt wird. Kurven und Körpervolumen sorgen für eine neue Dynamik und für Eigenschaften, die die Muster in der flächigen Gestaltung nicht vorweisen können.

Die hier zusammengestellten Musterthemen sind originell und innovativ. Es finden sich die unterschiedlichsten Motive, von Tischen, die in chaotischer Anordnung ein T-Shirt bedecken, über Hämmer und Schraubenschlüssel auf einem Kleid bis hin zu einem Eisberg, der vom Saum einer Hose aufzusteigen scheint. Daneben gibt es aber auch Gestaltungselemente, die sich nie ändern werden und deshalb ebenfalls bei der Auswahl berücksichtigt wurden: Streifen, Punkte, Paisley-Muster und Tiermotive sind geradezu unverwüstlich. Mit einer individuellen Gestaltung wecken sie unsere Aufmerksamkeit und geben Designklassikern einen neuen Touch, indem sie den Grundgedanken im Einsatz von Farben, Proportionen oder diversen Techniken variieren.

BLACK, GRAY AND WHITE
NOIR, GRIS ET BLANC
SCHWARZ, GRAU UND WEISS

Spring-summer 08 collection. Photo © Shoji Fujii; styling: Hannes Hetta; hair: Adrien Pinault; makeup: Patrice Graf

A spider's web; the fissures that appear when it has not rained for so long that the ground has dried and cracked; a vast stretch of land seen from above; the cracks on a plate after it has been broken and glued together again; the veins of an intricate leaf...

Une toile d'araignée, la surface du sol fissurée qui sèche et qui se brise après une longue période sans pluie, un vaste territoire vu du ciel, les « cicatrices » d'une assiette recollée après avoir été cassée, les nervures d'une feuille complexe…

Spinnennetz; ausgedörrte Erde, die nach langer Trockenheit aufgerissen ist; eine Landschaft aus der Vogelperspektive; „Narben" auf einem zerbrochenen Teller, der geklebt wurde; komplexe Blattadern …

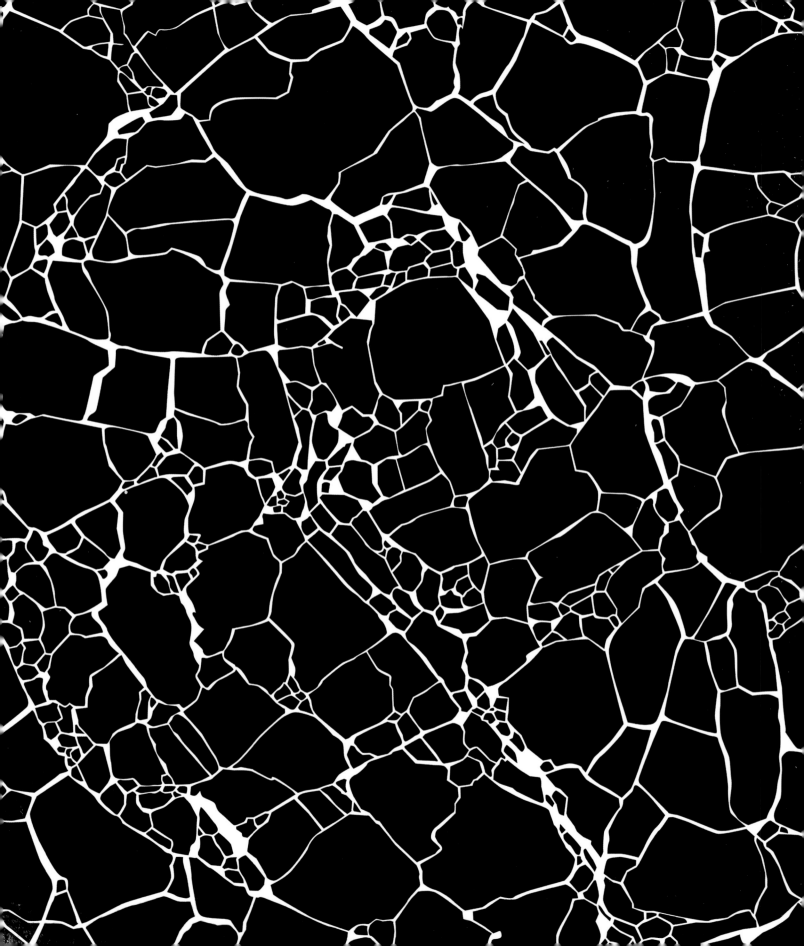

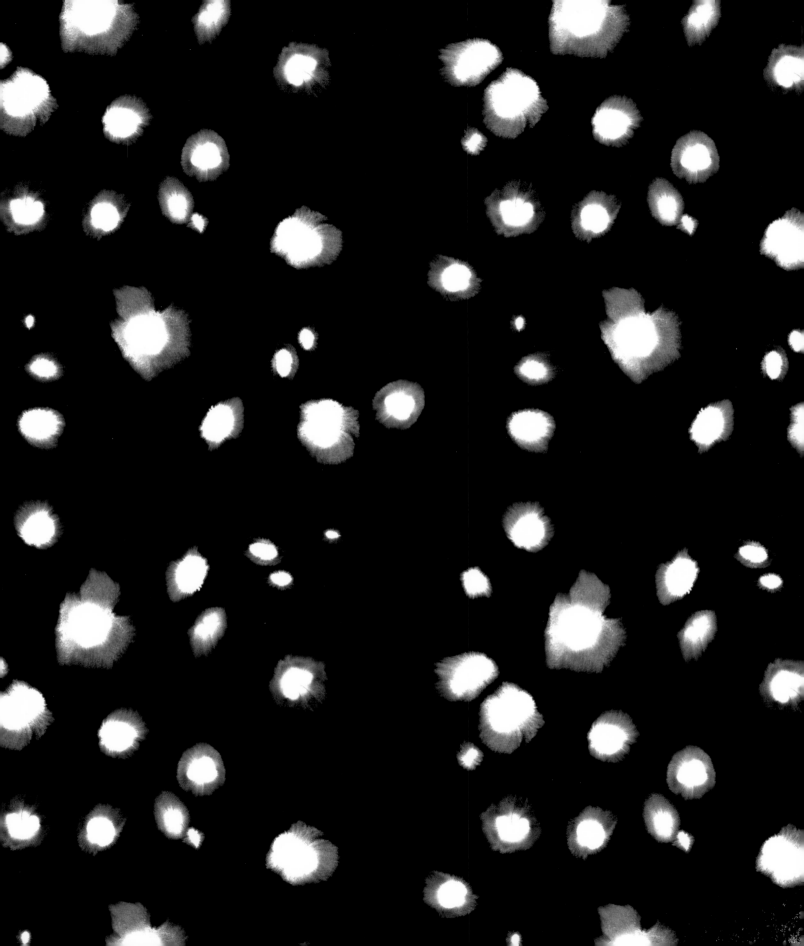

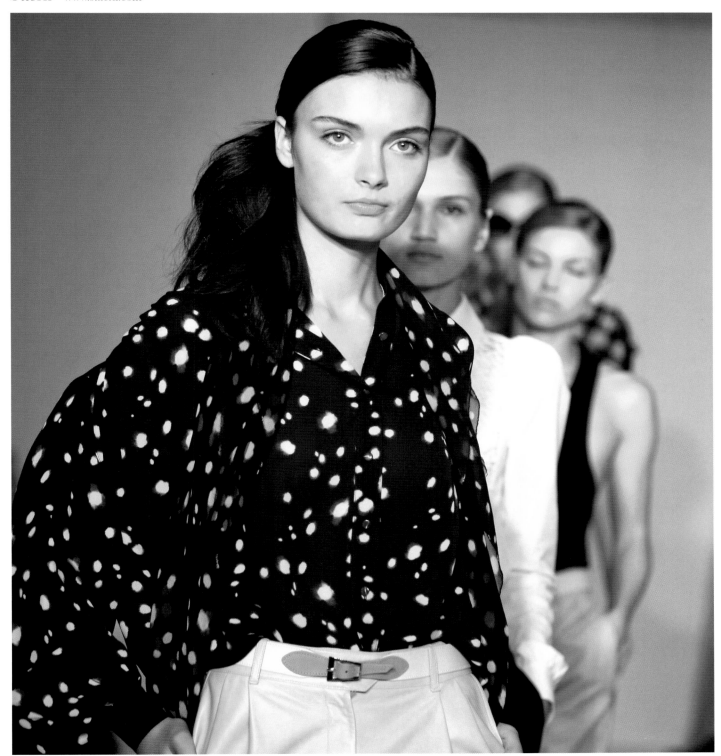

While this pattern recalls snowflakes falling on a cold winter's night, in fact it is the designer's personal take on the spots of a Dalmatian dog. To create this effect, black ink was dripped onto white paper and then the colors were reversed.

Ce qui ressemble à des flocons de neige par une froide nuit d'hiver est en fait une interprétation toute personnelle des taches du pelage d'un dalmatien. Pour les créer, on a laissé tomber des gouttes d'encre noire sur un papier blanc, puis inversé la combinaison de couleurs.

Schneeflocken in einer kalten Winternacht? Nein, eine Neuinterpretation der Flecken im Dalmatiner-fell. Hierfür ließ man schwarze Tinte auf ein weißes Blatt tropfen und kehrte dann die Farb-kombination um.

Rainy days and the cold make us long for our own four walls when far from home. Printed with the ARCHITECTONIC COAT pattern, this garment was specially designed for such days. It is intended to make the wearer feel as though she were in the comfort of her own home.

Lorsque l'on est loin de chez soi, le froid et les jours de pluie intensifient le mal du pays. Ce manteau, imprimé avec le motif ARCHITECTONIC COAT (manteau architectural), a été conçu pour ces moments en donnant à la personne qui le porte l'impression d'être comme à la maison.

In der Ferne verschlimmert sich Heimweh bei Kälte und an Regentagen. Eigens für solche Tage ist der Mantel mit dem Aufdruck ARCHITECTONIC COAT (Architektonischer Mantel) gedacht – in ihm fühlt man sich wie zu Hause.

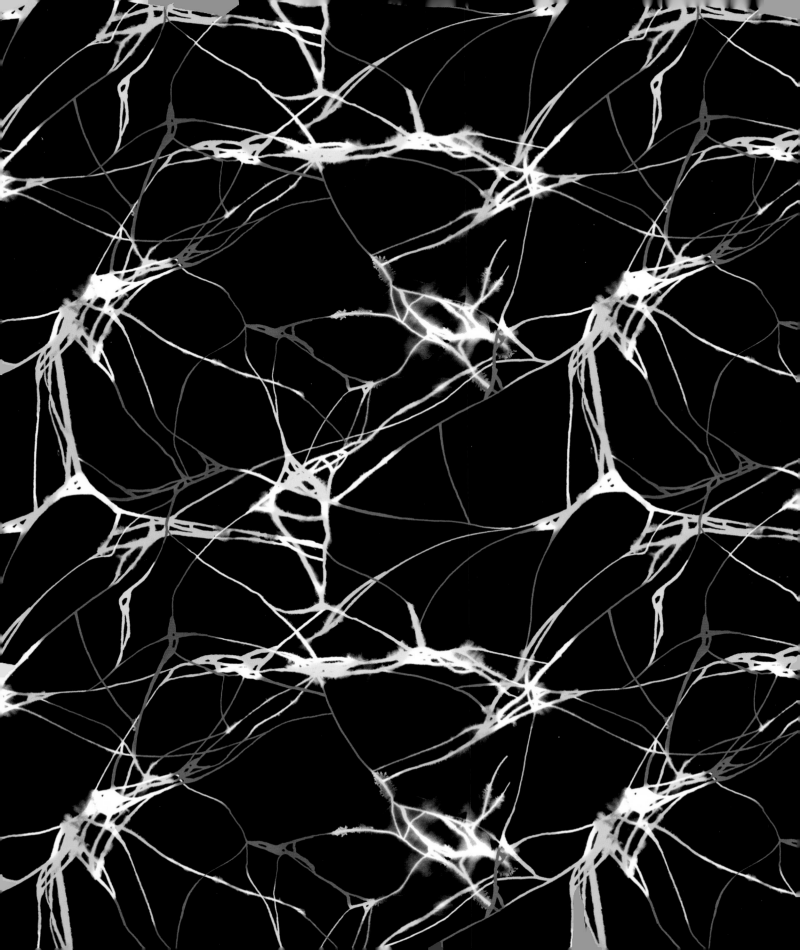

Karen Blixen (the Dane also known by her literary pseudonym Isak Dinesen), famous for her books in which she recounts her experiences in Africa, was the inspiration for this pattern, in which a two-tone pen-and-ink drawing covers a sheet of paper.

La Danoise Karen Blixen (également connue sous le pseudonyme littéraire d'Isak Dinesen), célèbre pour ses livres relatant ses expériences en Afrique, a inspiré ce motif où l'encre d'un dessin à la plume s'est répandue en deux tonalités sur un papier.

Die Dänin Karen Blixen, die auch unter dem Pseudonym Isak Dinesen bekannt ist, wurde mit Büchern über ihre Lebenserfahrungen in Afrika berühmt. Diese dienten als Inspiration für dieses Muster, das als Federzeichnung in zwei Farbtönen auf Papier angelegt wurde.

Native Americans used totem poles to link themselves to an object, animal or supernatural being, from which they believed they had descended and inherited certain attributes. Today, this new take on a totem pole unites people with a shared conviction: to follow potipoti.

Le totem servait de trait d'union entre une tribu et un objet, un être ou un animal surnaturel dont elle croyait descendre. À travers lui, la tribu recevait toutes ses qualités. Aujourd'hui, cette interprétation d'un totem unit un groupe à une même croyance : suivre potipoti.

Totems galten als Bindeglied zu übernatürlichen Gegenständen, Wesen oder Tieren, in denen Stämme ihre Ahnen sahen, und verkörpern spezielle Eigenschaften. Heute hat sich eine Gruppe Gleichgesinnter einem Totem verschrieben: Potipoti zu folgen.

Black tree silhouettes appear against a cold, gray concrete wall; their pointy branches cast monochrome shadows like eternal protests that recall the passing of time. This pattern is an urban jungle designed exclusively for this cult skater brand.

Des silhouettes noires de branches d'arbres sur un mur en béton gris et froid, des mois qui passent tandis que des bras effilés impriment les ombres monochromatiques de leurs éternelles révoltes. Une jungle urbaine conçue exclusivement pour cette marque fétiche des skateurs.

Schwarze Astsilhouetten vor einer kalten grauen Betonwand; Monate, in denen die Zeit verstreicht, während zarte Arme in ewigem Protest monochrome Schatten werfen. Ein urbaner Dschungel, der exklusiv für diese Skatermarke entworfen wurde.

Just like Native American totem poles, the model stands in a forest, as though she were the emblem of this fall–winter 2008 collection, which was indeed inspired by these traditional sculptures.

Tel un ancien totem d'Amérique du Nord, elle se dresse au milieu d'une forêt, comme s'il s'agissait de l'emblème de la collection automne-hiver 2008. Une collection qui s'inspire tout particulièrement de ces éléments durables et caractéristiques.

Wie ein nordamerikanisches Totem steht sie mitten im Wald – als handele es sich um das Emblem der Herbst-/Winterkollektion 2008. Tatsächlich wurde die Kollektion von uralten und markanten Stammeszeichen angeregt.

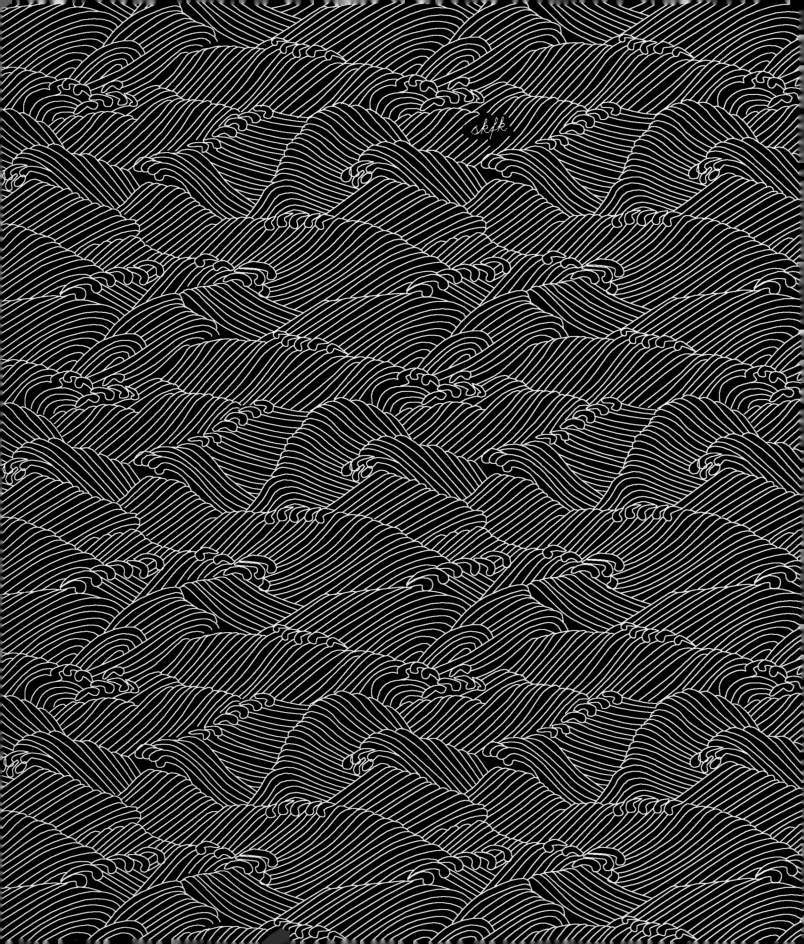

This pattern repeats waves ad infinitum, a bit like the illusionistic drawings of M. C. Escher. At certain points, the waves seem to recede and turn into clouds. The pattern has solid lines and appears to move, as if by the wind of a storm; it also includes thinner lines of a more Japanese aesthetic.

Comme dans les dessins impossibles d'Escher, ce motif est constitué de vagues incessantes. À un endroit, elles commencent à reculer et se transforment en nuages. Des lignes nettes, dont le mouvement semble provoqué par une tempête, s'allient à d'autres plus fines de style japonais.

Wie auf den Escher-Zeichnungen wiederholt dieses Muster unaufhörlich Wellen. Dort wo sie auf ein Hindernis treffen, verwandeln sie sich in Wolken. Kräftige, gewitterbewegte Striche sind mit feinen Linien kombiniert, die eher japanisch anmuten.

This pattern rethinks the iconic lotus petals used in yantra, presenting them as interconnecting geometric arches. As it is applied, the pattern is versatile and can be used on both larger and smaller scales, varying from the masculine abstract to childlike feminity.

Les emblématiques pétales de lotus employés par Yantra ont été revus et corrigés et se présentent comme des figures géométriques en forme d'arcs entrelacés. Ce motif est très variable dans son utilisation puisqu'il peut être employé à petite ou grande échelle, pour l'homme viril ou la femme-enfant.

Die in einem Yantra verwendeten Lotusblüten-blätter werden hier neu interpretiert und als geometrisch verschlungene Bögen dargestellt. Dieses vielseitige Muster kann im großen und kleinen Maßstab eingesetzt werden und variiert vom abstrakt Männlichen bis zum kindlich Weiblichen.

FALL 2008

This pattern recalls simple doodling on paper with a felt-tip pen, something schoolchildren are known to do while listening distractedly to their teachers. This pastime has now become a widespread source of shirt patterns.

Ce motif pour tee-shirts, qui évoque une activité aussi banale et courante de notre enfance que le griffonnage sur un bout de papier pour combler l'ennui pendant les explications des professeurs à l'école, est aujourd'hui vendu à grande échelle.

Früher kritzelten wir in langweiligen Schulstunden doch alle mit dem Stift auf einem Blatt Papier herum. Etwas so Einfaches und Alltägliches hat sich hier – in großem Maßstab – in ein T-Shirt-Muster verwandelt.

Ndeur   www.ndeur.com

When creating a new design, this artist generally combines a variety of patterns from different historical and artistic periods, be they classic, ethnic or more modern. This gives rise to truly unique designs.

Le travail de cet artiste se base principalement sur la combinaison d'une grande variété de motifs issus de diverses périodes historiques et artistiques, regroupant indistinctement des motifs classiques, ethniques et d'autres plus modernes, pour créer un style propre.

Der Grundgedanke des Künstlers war, eine große Mustervielfalt – egal ob klassisch, Ethno oder modern – aus mehreren historischen und künstlerischen Zeiträumen zu kombinieren, um daraus seinen eigenen Entwurf zu schaffen.

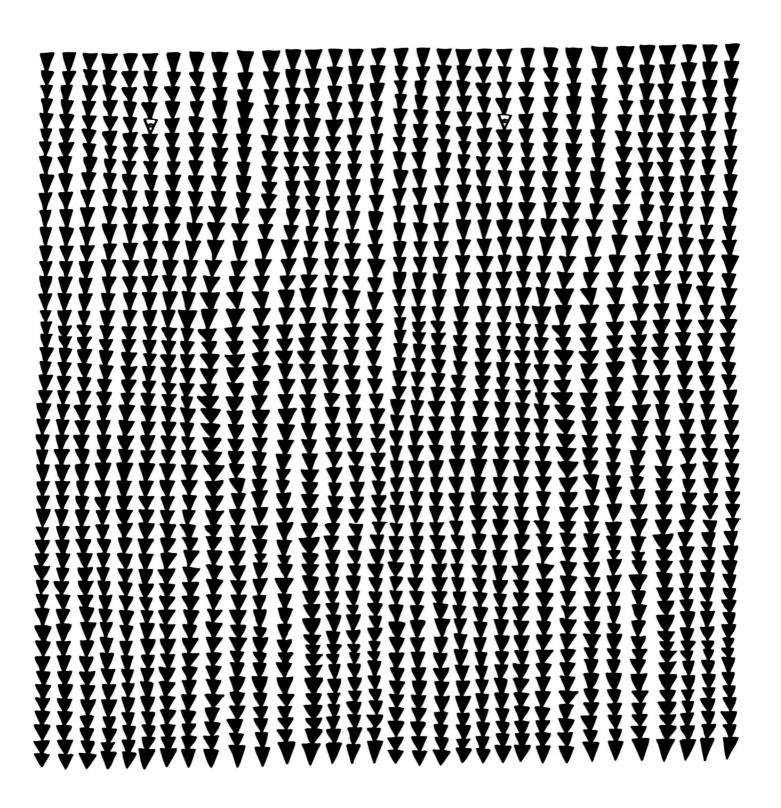

Thousands of mini mountains were hand-drawn for this pattern. The mountains are irregular both in terms of their size and arrangement in rows, creating an interesting—and somewhat dizzying—effect, and a visual interplay between figure and background.

Des milliers de petites montagnes ont été dessinées à la main pour ce motif. Irrégulières aussi bien par leur taille que par leur agencement en rangées, ces formes créent un effet visuel intéressant (et parfois même étourdissant) qui joue avec la figure et le fond.

Für dieses Schwindel erregende Muster wurden tausende kleine Berge per Hand gezeichnet. Sie variieren innerhalb der Reihungen in der Größe und Anordnung, sodass ein interessanter optischer Effekt entsteht, der mit Formen und Hintergrund spielt.

Thousands of insects creep and crawl over this design, which, incidentally, is not under copyright, meaning that it can be used by anyone for anything. So, just like in early horror films, this pattern of insects could just take over the world.

Des milliers d'insectes grouillent sur ce dessin libre de droits de reproduction, et que n'importe qui peut utiliser à sa guise. Par analogie, il est alors facile d'imaginer, comme dans les vieux films d'horreur, que le motif pourrait, à l'instar des insectes, dominer le monde.

Tausende Insekten vereinen sich hier zu einem Muster. Es ist rechtefrei und darf beliebig verwendet werden. Daraus ergibt sich leicht die Analogie, dass Muster – ähnlich wie Insekten in alten Horrorfilmen – einmal die Welt beherrschen werden.

This pattern was inspired by the countless stories and urban myths that surround any drive-in restaurant in LA, such as the story of a psychedelic waitress who slowly and sensually moves toward a car, ready to realize all the hungry driver's dreams.

Ce motif s'inspire des innombrables histoires et légendes qui entourent les services de restauration en voiture de L.A., comme celle où une serveuse psychédélique s'approche lentement et sensuellement de la voiture pour satisfaire tous les désirs du conducteur affamé.

Dieses Muster ist von unzähligen Geschichten und Fantasien inspiriert, die um Drive-in-Restaurants in L.A. kreisen, wo sich die psychedelische Kellnerin langsam und verführerisch dem Auto nähert, um alle Träume des hungrigen Fahrers zu verwirklichen.

Drawing with a felt-tip pen is always the same, yet a different effect is created when using different pens. Here, thick snaking lines cover broad strokes that seem to beat out a rhythm, while the background is marked by thin, cursory strokes.

Écrire avec un seul marqueur ne donne rien de surprenant, mais le résultat est bien différent si l'on en utilise plusieurs. Ici, de larges traits enroulés en spirales cachent un tracé presque compulsif qui semble marquer un rythme, sur un fond de fines lignes impulsives.

Das Malen mit einem Filzstift ist immer gleich, aber mit unterschiedlichen Stiften ändert sich auch das Ergebnis. Hier sind satte Kringel auf breite Striche gesetzt, die den Rhythmus vorgeben, und daneben erscheinen feine, spontan gesetzte Linien.

Delicate female silhouettes have been screenprinted by hand onto a silk jacket that combines two shades of silver. The lines of the figures flow smoothly into one another, creating new shapes and textures—even in the gaps—and an attractive pattern.

Cette veste en soie, qui conjugue deux tons argentés, présente les sérigraphies de délicates silhouettes de femme. Les lignes des silhouettes s'entremêlent avec fluidité pour composer de nouvelles formes et textures jusque dans les vides, créant ainsi un motif original.

Zarte Frauensilhouetten wurden im Siebdruck per Hand auf diese Seidenjacke aufgetragen, die zwei Silbertöne kombiniert. Die ineinander verfließenden Figurenkonturen lassen an einzelnen Stellen neue Formen und Texturen entstehen und ergeben dabei ein interessantes Muster.

This sweatshirt is printed with images of silver paper. The design is based on the thin silver suits and hats that some sci-fi buffs use as a way of protecting themselves against alien frequencies, electromagnetic fields, and mind reading and control.

Ce sweat-shirt imprimé d'images en papier d'aluminium fait songer aux combinaisons et aux chapeaux à fine texture portés par certaines personnes pour se protéger des fréquences extraterrestres, des champs électromagnétiques et éviter que l'on contrôle et lise leurs pensées.

Das mit Abbildungen von Folien bedruckte Sweat-shirt verweist auf dünne Anzüge und Hüte aus Alufolie, wie sie getragen werden, um sich gegen die Frequenzen außerirdischer Wesen, elektro-magnetische Felder, die Kontrolle und das Lesen von Gedanken zu schützen.

Ndeur www.ndeur.com

The pattern on these shoes—of which 20 pairs were made on special order from a San Diego gallery—bears some resemblance to cherry blossom. This is because it is inspired by a modern take on Japanese culture and on kimonos.

Le motif imprimé sur ces baskets (une commande spéciale de 20 paires pour une galerie à San Diego) rappelle les fleurs du cerisier puisque son design s'inspire de la culture japonaise et des kimonos, interprétés dans une optique moderne.

Dieses Muster war ein Sonderauftrag für 20 Turnschuhe für eine Galerie in San Diego. Es hat eine gewisse Ähnlichkeit mit Kirschblüten und beruht auf einer neuen Wahrnehmung von japanischer Kultur und Kimonos.

SCHOOL FURNITURE shows the chaos that would ensue if, during a break in the school year, when no one is watching the empty classrooms, chairs and tables were to reveal their true nature by forming opposing groups, with no fear of being seen by human eyes.

SCHOOL FURNITURE (mobilier scolaire) montre le désordre qui règnerait dans les salles de classe abandonnées lors d'une calme journée de vacances, si les chaises et les tables décidaient de se rebeller, de s'allier, de s'affronter sans craindre le regard de l'homme...

SCHOOL FURNITURE (Schulmöbel) demonstriert das Chaos, das entstehen würde, wenn Stühle und Tische an einem ruhigen Ferientag, an dem die Klassenräume unbewacht sind, rebellierten, Banden gründeten und gegen den Menschen aufbegehrten.

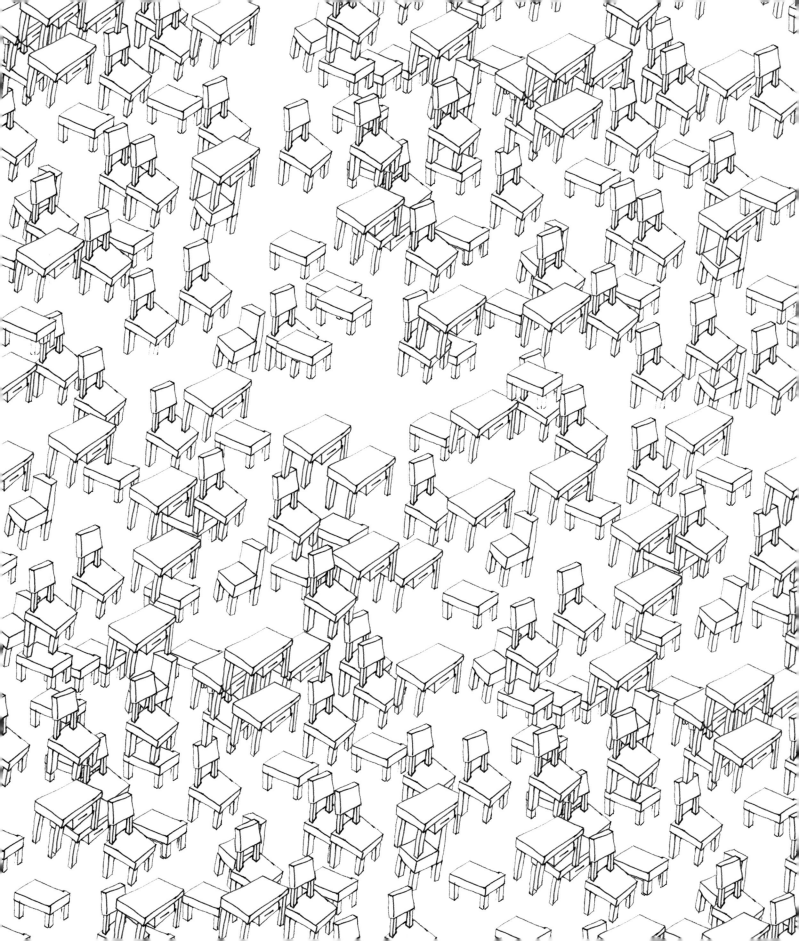

The desire to be protected has increased due to the global situation of recent years. BOMBAS EXPLOTANDO (exploding bombs) aims to convey the importance of being protected, with nothing and nobody being able to harm us, not even poisonous green or deathly black.

Par les temps qui courent, se sentir protégé se révèle de plus en plus important. BOMBAS EXPLOTANDO (explosion de bombes) veut faire comprendre l'importance de se sentir protéger, sans que rien ni personne ne puisse nous faire du mal, pas même le vert venin ni le noir couleur de mort.

Weltweit hat das Thema Sicherheit in den letzten Jahren an Bedeutung gewonnen. BOMBAS EXPLOTANDO (Explodierende Bomben) will aufzeigen, wie wichtig Schutz für uns ist und dass wir durch nichts und niemanden Schaden nehmen – weder durch Umweltgifte noch durch Anschläge.

This pattern has a simple recipe: find a shirt to match your 70s-style van, add a topographical map, blend at top speed, add a pinch of optical illusion, and then chill. Best served on a black or white background.

Une recette simple pour ce motif : trouver une chemise assortie à votre van des années 70, ajouter une carte routière, passer au mixer à pleine puissance, ajouter une pincée d'illusion d'optique et laisser refroidir. Pour une meilleure présentation, servir sur fond noir ou blanc.

Ein Muster mit einfachem Rezept: Man nehme ein Hemd aus den 1970er-Jahren und eine topografische Karte und verrühre alles bei höchster Geschwindigkeit. Dazu eine Prise Optik. Abkühlen lassen. Auf schwarzem oder weißem Hintergrund servieren.

Yiyí Gutz
www.yiyigutz.es

CALAVERITAS (little skulls), a characteristic symbol of danger, is part of a collection that is essentially concerned with protecting both our exteriors and interiors. This is what we fight to achieve every day: full immunity, which is the very paradigm of the body's triumph.

CALAVERITAS (têtes de mort). Symbole de danger, elles font partie d'une collection consacrée avant tout à la protection, aussi bien de l'extérieur que de l'intérieur, pour laquelle nous luttons chaque jour afin d'atteindre l'immunité totale, qui n'est autre que le paradigme du triomphe du corps.

CALAVERITAS (Totenköpfe) als Sinnbild für Gefahr zeichnen diese Kollektion aus, die sich innere und äußere Sicherheit zum Thema gemacht hat. Sie verweisen auf das Paradigma des täglichen Kampfs um vollständigen und allumfassenden Schutz.

The clubs and spades in this pattern indicate that the design is based on gambling. The theory says that, to achieve our dreams, we must take risks. We need to gamble without relying on chance: we must be good strategists and always have an ace up our sleeves.

Ce motif qui représente les quatre couleurs du jeu de cartes, s'inspire des jeux de hasard. Il faut prendre des risques pour accomplir ses rêves, paraît-il. Il faut donc jouer sans rien attendre du hasard et se comporter en un fin stratège, en cachant un as dans sa manche.

Das Muster entstammt den Farben von Spielkarten. Nach der Theorie muss man Risiken wagen, damit Träume wahr werden können. Und so riskiert man seinen Einsatz, ohne sich aber auf den Zufall zu verlassen – auch ein guter Stratege braucht ein As im Ärmel.

YELLOW, RED AND PINK
JAUNE, ROUGE ET ROSE
GELB, ROT UND ROSA

One fine day, a man bought a bunch of chrysanthemums for his home—purple flowers with a yellow center. He placed them in the parlor, where he had a reading lamp with a stripy colored shade. THE HANDSOME is a pattern based on these two elements when viewed together.

Un jour, quelqu'un acheta un bouquet de chrysanthèmes lilas et jaunes pour sa maison et le posa dans le salon, où se trouvait une liseuse avec un écran à rayures de couleurs. La combinaison de ces deux éléments constitue la base de THE HANDSOME (le beau).

Jemand kaufte für seine Wohnung einmal einen Strauß lila Chrysanthemen mit gelbem Blütenherz und stellte ihn ins Wohnzimmer. Dort stand eine Leselampe mit bunt gestreiftem Lampenschirm. Der Anblick beider Elemente wurde zum Anlass für THE HANDSOME (Der Gutaussehende).

CRAZY MONKEYS is based on a true story: a close encounter of the third kind between Alexandre, the designer, and a monkey in the rainforest on the island of Sumatra. This pattern immortalizes the night when he touched the monkey's fingers and received its cold gaze.

CRAZY MONKEYS (singes fous) est basé sur une histoire vraie : une rencontre du troisième type entre Alexandre (son créateur) et un singe dans la jungle de l'île de Sumatra. Comment oublier le contact de ses doigts et le regard glacial qu'il lui lança cette nuit-là...

CRAZY MONKEYS (Verrückte Affen) beruht auf einem wirklichen Ereignis: einer Begegnung zwischen dem Designer Alexandre und einem Affen im tropischen Urwald der Insel Sumatra. Er wird den Blick in jener Nacht nie vergessen und wie seine Finger ihn berührt haben ...

The creator of One Teaspoon has a long-standing fascination with the classic Paisley pattern. The team therefore constantly seeks ways of reinventing it. And this time, the result is rather complex, although its colors and balance mean the pattern does not cause visual overload.

Le créateur de One Teaspoon étant depuis longtemps obsédé par le motif de paisley, son équipe cherche en permanence à réinventer le dessin. Ici, le résultat est assez complexe, même si grâce à son équilibre et aux couleurs choisies il ne sature pas la vue.

Der Schöpfer von One Teaspoon ist schon seit langem wie besessen vom klassischen Paisley-Muster; sein Team sucht daher stets nach Möglichkeiten, es neu zu erfinden. Hier ist das Ergebnis äußerst komplex, aber dank der Symmetrie und Farben wirkt das Muster nicht überladen.

In Arabic calligraphy, Kufic is the oldest-known style. It is characterized by sharp angles and rectangular shapes. Kufic script, which today is still one of the most popular styles, is the source of inspiration for this design.

Le style connu le plus ancien de la calligraphie arabe est le coufique, caractérisé, en règle générale, par des angles très prononcés et des formes carrées. Aujourd'hui encore très utilisé, il constitue la source d'inspiration de ce motif.

Der kufische Stil ist der älteste bekannte Stil der arabischen Kalligrafie und zeichnet sich durch markante Konturen und eine geometrische Linienführung aus. Heute noch ist er sehr beliebt und diente auch als Anregung für diesen Entwurf.

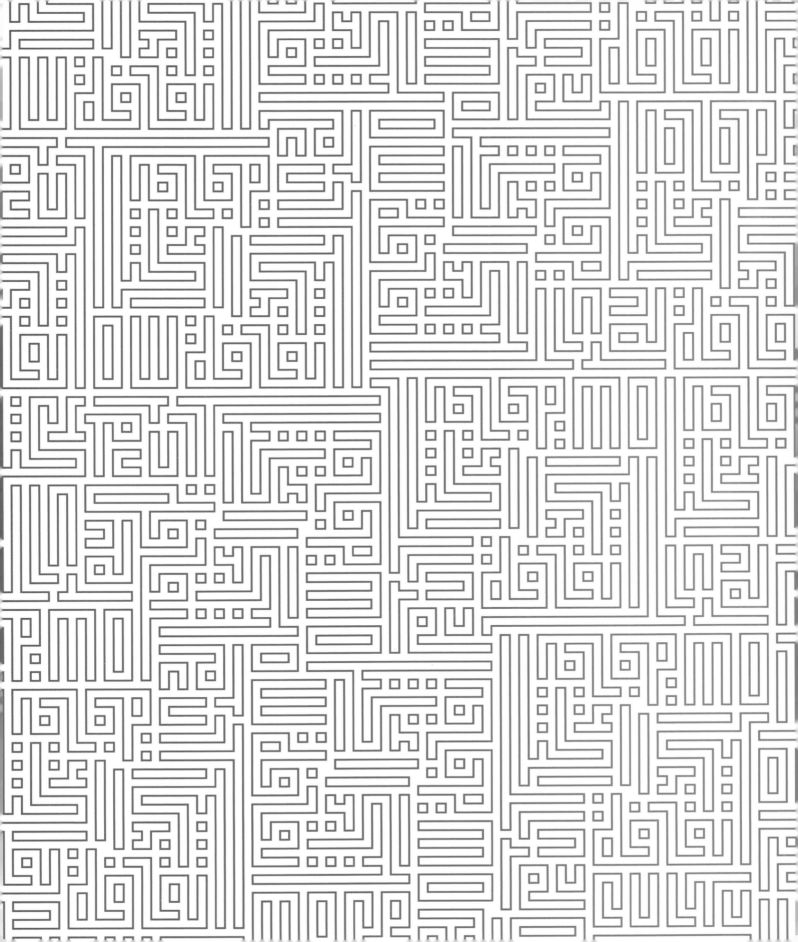

© Ingen Frygt

Kirsty is the imaginary muse of the creator of this pattern, who likes working in a psychedelic, romantic garden, which has provided the inspiration for this unique version of a floral pattern. It is actually the silhouette of a colored remnant with flowers.

Kirsty est la muse imaginaire de la créatrice de ce design. Elle aime travailler dans un jardin psychédélique et romantique, source d'inspiration de cette vision toute personnelle d'un motif fleuri. Un motif qui représente les contours d'un morceau coloré de tissu à fleurs.

Kirsty ist die Fantasiemuse der Schöpferin. Sie liebt die Arbeit in einem romantischen Garten, der sie zur Gestaltung des psychedelischen Blumenmusters anregte. Tatsächlich war die Silhouette ein Stoffrest mit einem bunten Blumenmuster.

Color is a great reason to love the fall. This pattern is inspired by this time of the year and makes use of its characteristic color explosion to recreate a pile of dying leaves. Furthermore, smaller leaves are used to add texture and depth to the leaf on the top.

La couleur nous donne une raison d'aimer l'automne. Ce motif, inspiré de cette période de l'année, réutilise l'explosion de couleurs qui caractérise l'automne. Au milieu d'un tapis de feuilles surgissent, ici et là, de plus petites, sur le point de faner, auxquelles le designer a donné plus de texture et de profondeur.

Farbe charakterisiert den Herbst – daher mögen wir ihn. Dieses Muster, von der herbstlichen Farbenexplosion inspiriert, verwendet viele kleine Blätter, um einem jeweils fast verwelkten, größeren Blatt Textur und Tiefe zu geben.

This pattern, comprising images of colorful toy trucks, is mainly used for retro-style undies for kids, and for long johns. It is intended as an expression of individuality and to encourage people to play with the limits of fashion, and to avoid being conventional and predictable.

Les sous-vêtements rétro pour enfants et les caleçons longs sont les principales références de ce motif aux camions miniatures colorés, qui vise à encourager les gens à s'exprimer et à jouer un peu avec les limites de la mode, pour ne pas tomber dans le conformisme et l'ennui.

Bunte Spielzeuglaster sind Grundlage für dieses Muster, das für Kinderunterwäsche und lange Unterhosen im Retrolook bestimmt ist. Hier kann sich der Träger ausdrücken und mit den Grenzen der Mode spielen, um dem Konventionellen und Banalen zu entgehen.

These anatomical hearts, each pierced by an arrow, bring to mind the suffering we can feel when in love—not falling out of love. Love is a deep emotion, so it can be painful. Sometimes it can even cause the spillage of blood, which, perhaps not by chance, shares the same color as passion: red.

Ces cœurs anatomiques, transpercés d'une flèche, représentent la souffrance que l'on ressent lorsque l'on est amoureux (pas lors d'un chagrin d'amour), car ce sentiment est si profond qu'il peut s'avérer très douloureux et faire jaillir du sang rouge, couleur de la passion.

Die von einem Pfeil durchbohrten Herzen stehen für das Leid, das Verliebte empfinden – aber nicht wegen dem Verlust der Liebe. Ein solches Gefühl ist manchmal so tief, dass es schmerzt und das Herz zu bluten scheint – deshalb das Rot hier als Farbe der Leidenschaft.

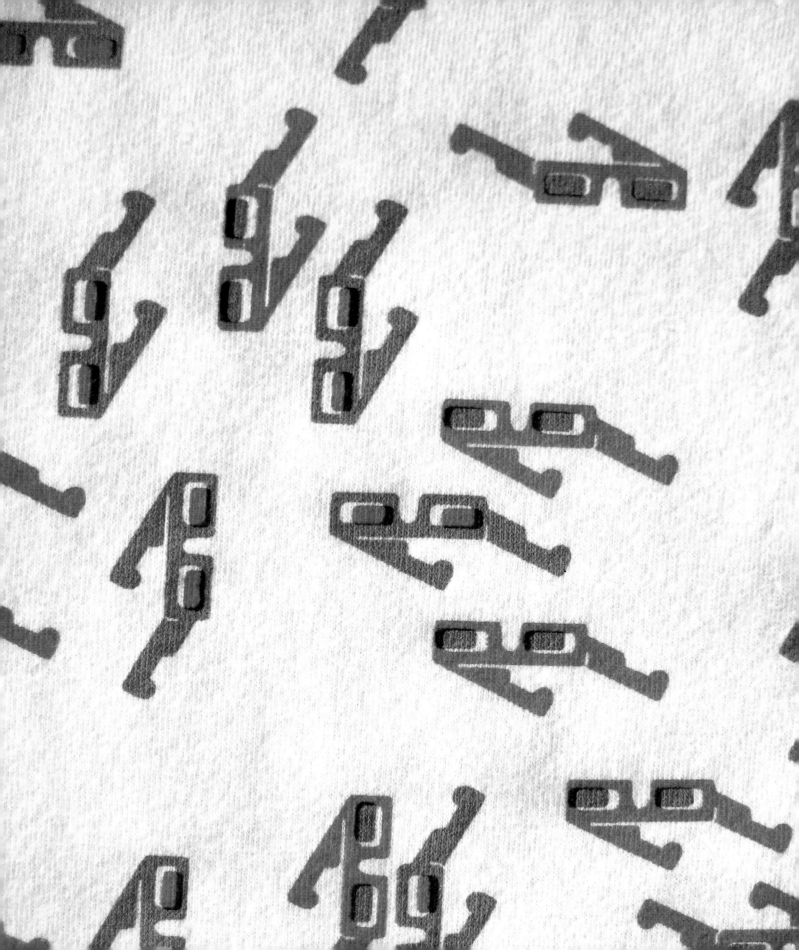

Clea Garrick (Limedrop)   www.limedrop.com.au

Collection: *All 3 Dimensions* © Jeph Ko, www.jephko.com; hair: Emma Savige; makeup: Jess Crema

This pattern was designed to be viewed with 3D glasses. Both garments use the same Pantone numbers in their colors, making the image of the pattern vibrate slightly. In trying to focus, the eye is deceived by the colors, which make the pattern appear to move.

Ce motif a été conçu pour être regardé avec des lunettes 3D. Ces deux modèles utilisent la même référence de couleur Pantone, ce qui fait légèrement trembler l'image du motif. Lors de la mise au point, les couleurs trompent l'œil et accentuent cette sensation de mouvement.

Dieses Muster wurde für das Betrachten mit 3-D-Brille geschaffen. Beide Motive verwenden für ihre Farben die gleiche Pantonenummer, sodass das Muster leicht zu vibrieren scheint. Beim Fokussieren wird das Auge von den Farben getäuscht – es entsteht ein Eindruck von Bewegung.

This original pattern with an undeniable gypsy style was inspired by the raucous wedding in Emir Kusturica's movie *Black Cat, White Cat*. Typical elements have been juxtaposed as a collage that boasts the feel and contemporary style of Helgason.

Ce motif original, d'un style clairement gitan, est inspiré du mariage tumultueux du film *Chat noir, chat blanc* d'Emir Kusturica. Les éléments typiques ont été juxtaposés, à la manière d'un collage, au style particulier et contemporain de Helgason.

Das originelle Muster mit der unverkennbaren Zigeuneroptik orientiert sich an der schrillen Hochzeit in Emir Kusturicas Film *Schwarze Katze, weißer Kater*. Die charakteristischen Elemente wurden mit dem für Helgason typischen modernen Stil collageartig nebeneinandergesetzt.

Created with subtlety and hints of nostalgia, FLOWER BOMB looks like a windmill in which soft flower petals, which seem to emanate from a strong and contrasting core, flutter in the wind.

Conçu à partir de subtiles références nostalgiques, FLOWER BOMB (bombe à fleur) rappelle un moulin à vent dont les légers pétales de fleurs réalisés à l'encre, paraissant issus d'un élément géométrique solide et en contraste, sont fouettés par le vent.

FLOWER BOMB (Blumenbombe) wurde mit subtilen nostalgischen Bezügen entwickelt. Das Muster ähnelt einem Windrad aus zarten, mit Tinte gezeichneten Blüten, die von einem kontrastreichen und stark geometrischen Element auszugehen scheinen und vom Wind gepeitscht werden.

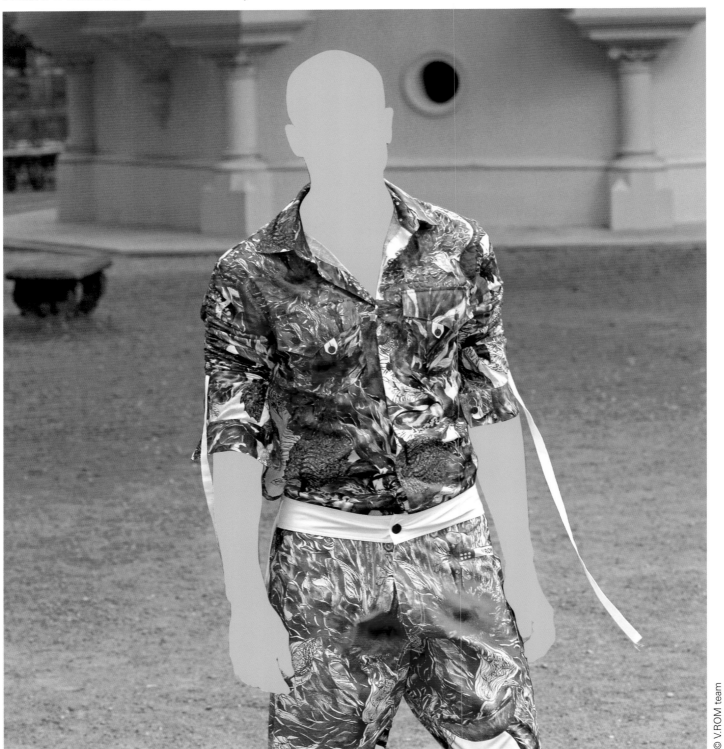

The summer of 2007 and the amazing and diverse flora of Brazil—with its carnival of lush colors and delicate lines—provided the inspiration for the pattern printed on these garments, which illustrates aromatic hibiscus, recognizable by its long, slender pistil.

Été 2007, la flore brésilienne si étonnante et variée (avec son carnaval de couleurs exubérantes et de lignes délicates) est à l'origine de la conception du motif imprimé sur ces vêtements, ornés d'hibiscus aromatiques, reconnaissables à leur pistil fin et allongé.

Die beeindruckende brasilianische Flora mit ihren üppigen Farben und feinen Linien war Muster-grundlage für diese Kleidungsstücke vom Sommer 2007. Man erkennt duftende Hibiskus-blüten mit langen, dünnen Stempeln.

This illustration is part of a series based on the marine aesthetics of caravels, represented through its illustrator's dreamlike vision. Here, one evening just when the sun is about to disappear, its magical golden light accompanies these ancient vessels.

Ce dessin fait partie d'une série basée sur l'esthétique marine des caravelles, vue à travers le regard onirique propre à l'illustratrice. Le soleil, qui est ici sur le point de se coucher, plonge les vieilles embarcations dans sa lumière magique et dorée.

Das Motiv gehört zu einer Serie von Meeresansichten mit Karavellen, die der Traumwelt der Illustratorin entstammen. Hier sieht man alte Schiffe in der Dämmerung, während die untergehende Sonne ein zauberhaftes goldenes Licht wirft.

This pattern was designed with its later use in mind: a wrap skirt that, when worn, has a constantly changing aspect. The spots represent flower petals on a background that gradually turns from pink to green to dark gray.

Ce motif a été conçu dans l'optique de son utilisation ultérieure : une jupe portefeuille dont l'apparence doit constamment changer une fois mise en place. Les points ressemblent à des pétales de fleur sur un fond qui passe graduellement du rose au vert et au marengo.

Das Muster wurde eigens im Hinblick auf die spätere Nutzung des Kleidungsstücks entworfen: Es ziert einen Wickelrock, dessen Aussehen ständig wechseln soll, wenn er geschlossen ist. Die Punkte wirken wie Blütenblätter auf einem Hintergrund, der allmählich von Rosa zu Grün und dann zu Dunkelgrau wechselt.

This pattern is the result of a love triangle between African tribal jewelry, totem poles and traditional Indonesian architecture. When choosing the colors, the designer opted to use the feminine colors of stone pink and pastel grape, applied with a subtle graded effect.

Ce motif est le fruit d'un trio amoureux entre la joaillerie tribale africaine, les totems et l'architecture traditionnelle indonésienne. Le choix des couleurs vise à faire ressortir un côté féminin, le rose et le lilas étant appliqués avec un délicat effet de dégradé.

Das Muster ist das Ergebnis einer Dreiecksbeziehung zwischen afrikanischem Stammesschmuck, Totems und traditioneller indonesischer Architektur. Bei der Auswahl der Farben entschied man sich mit dezent nuanciertem Rosa und Lila für eine feminine Note.

Amy Lou Bilodeau amylouxo@lycos.com

One of the things that most fascinate this designer is the mystical essence related in Native American mythology. This pattern therefore features a unique version of an element illustrated in these tales: different-sized scales of chevrons and feathers.

L'essence mystique est l'un des aspects de la mythologie des Indiens d'Amérique les plus appréciés par cette créatrice. Elle a donc conçu ce motif de façon à créer une version unique d'un élément illustré par ces histoires. Il lui a permis de jouer avec les tailles de chevrons et de plumes.

Was die Designerin an der Mythologie der nord-amerikanischen Indianer so fasziniert, sind mystische Wesen. Daher entwarf sie dieses Muster, bei dem sie mit Farb- und Formenvariationen spielt, um die illustrierte Version einer Legende zu erschaffen.

HOJAS RAYAS (line leaves) simulates the structure of leaves, as if the wind blew so hard that only their veins remain. To enhance the pattern's lightness and delicacy, it was printed onto very fine cotton garments and soft colors were used.

HOJAS RAYAS (feuilles rayures) simule la structure de feuilles résistantes, dont seules les nervures auraient subsisté après une violente rafale. L'utilisation de couleurs douces et l'impression sur un tissu en coton fin ont permis d'accentuer l'effet de légèreté et la subtilité du motif.

HOJAS RAYAS simuliert komponierte Blattformen – als hätte der Wind so stark geweht, dass nur die Blattadern übrig blieben. Leichtigkeit und Feinheit des Musters zeigen sich in den zarten Farben und werden durch den Druck auf sehr dünne Baumwolle noch verstärkt.

Relating experiences is not easy: when something is subjective, it may be incomprehensible to others. It is therefore unlikely that you would guess that this pattern was inspired by an evening the designer spent in Berlin watching a sky full of fireworks while eating bratwurst and French fries.

Le vécu n'est pas facile à exprimer en raison de sa subjectivité, que les autres peuvent avoir du mal à comprendre. Ou… distingue-t-on ici clairement une nuit berlinoise au cours de laquelle des feux d'artifice remplissent le ciel tandis que je tiens une saucisse-frites dans les mains ?

Erlebnisse auszudrücken ist nicht immer einfach, wenn es sich um subjektive Erfahrungen handelt, die für andere unverständlich sind. Vielleicht erkennen Sie hier ein Feuerwerk am Nachthimmel über Berlin, während ich eine Bratwurst mit Pommes in den Händen halte?

This designer created a new version of paisley after studying the pattern itself—a great example of creativity and versatility—and traditional Russian handicrafts. In this design, the creator's imaginary muse Kirsty has been captured and hidden in the pattern.

L'étude de l'artisanat populaire russe et du motif paisley (exemple type de créativité et de versatilité) ont amené cette créatrice à réaliser une nouvelle version de ce motif. Elle y a capturée sa muse imaginaire Kirsty qui se trouve dissimulée entre divers éléments.

Nachdem die Designerin die russische Volkskunst und das Paisley-Muster erkundet hatte, demonstrierte sie deren Kreativität und Vielseitigkeit in einer persönlichen Interpretation. Hier wurde wieder die imaginäre Muse Kirsty eingefangen und in einigen Elementen verborgen.

© Olivia Hemus

The CLOUD PRINT pattern gives us an opportunity to explore one of those places that can be only vaguely recognized, probably because it was just a hazy dream. These are misty landscapes that are repeated time and again in the fabric of dresses and tops.

Le motif CLOUD PRINT (impression de nuage) nous offre la possibilité d'explorer l'un de ces endroits vaguement connus, probablement issus d'un rêve dont on se souvient à peine. Ces paysages embrumés sont reproduits encore et encore sur le tissu de robes et de hauts.

Das Muster CLOUD PRINT (Wolkendruck) bietet die Möglichkeit, kaum fassbare Orte auszuloten, die nicht aus der Erinnerung, sondern wohl aus Träumen aufsteigen. Nebelverhüllte Landschaften wiederholen sich beständig auf dem Stoff von Kleidern und Tops.

To set itself apart from classic checked prints while maintaining its roots in the basics of textile motifs, CHECKMATE has focused on using unconventionally sized squares as well as alternating colors and organic repetitions.

Afin de se distinguer du motif classique à carreaux, CHECKMATE (échec et mat) se concentre sur la taille peu habituelle de ses carreaux, le choix des couleurs et la fréquence de répétition de ceux-ci, même s'il cherche à conserver l'essence des motifs textiles de base.

Anders als das klassische Karomuster konzentriert sich CHECKMATE (Schachmatt) auf die ungewöhnliche Größe der Karos, die Farbauswahl und den Rhythmus, mit dem sich die Karos wiederholen, und bleibt dabei dennoch im Grundmuster verwurzelt.

VIOLET, BLUE AND GREEN
VIOLET, BLEU ET VERT
VIOLETT, BLAU UND GRÜN

Summer days, sunshades and sun terraces: this is one description of hours spent in a small, fragile shelter, watching how the sun's rays fall on the slopes, leaving thousands of ephemeral delineations in its wake while the heat becomes less intense, if only for a few hours.

Jours d'été, parasols et vérandas… Une synthèse personnelle des heures passées sous un petit abri fragile, au travers duquel passent les rayons du soleil, laissant sur leur passage des milliers de dessins éphémères, alors que la chaleur s'atténue, l'espace de quelques heures…

Sommertage, Sonnenschirme, Badeplätze … Eine persönliche Synthese der Stunden, die man unter einem fragilen Schutz verbringt, bis die Sonne wieder sinkt. Es verweilen flüchtige Zeichnungen, während das Licht für wenige Stunden seine Intensität verliert.

This is the first time the ONTOUR studio has invited an artist to work with them. They chose Cosmic Crack—a cosmic genre expert—who based this pattern on his countless pen doodles on arms, paper and drink coasters.

C'est la première fois que les créateurs du studio ONTOUR invitent un artiste à travailler avec eux. L'heureux élu, Cosmic Crack, s'est inspiré pour ce motif des innombrables dessins qu'il réalise au stylo-bille sur du papier, des dessous de verres ou des bras.

Das Studio ONTOUR hat erstmals einen Künstler um eine Zusammenarbeit gebeten. Der Auserwählte ist Cosmic Crack, der als Grundlage für dieses Muster die unzähligen Zeichnungen verwendete, die er mit Kugelschreiber auf Papiere, Glasuntersetzer oder Arme malt.

Styles as diverse as Art Deco and the opulent glamour of old theaters were the inspiration for POLKA DOT WAVE. The pattern revives Art Deco's symmetry and colors, which were used in the large and majestic velvet stage curtains of old theaters.

POLKA DOT WAVE (vague de pois) s'inspire de styles aussi variés que l'Art déco et le glamour opulent des anciens théâtres. Le premier apporte sa symétrie et son utilisation des couleurs, qui servaient à représenter les grands rideaux somptueux en velours.

POLKA DOT WAVE (Punktwelle) ist von mehreren Kunststilen und dem opulenten Glamour alter Theater angeregt. Vom Art déco werden Symmetrie und Farbeinsatz übernommen und für die Darstellung großer, majestätischer Samtvorhänge verwendet.

© Six 6 Photography

Chemical spirals as large as the universe or as small as molecules under a microscope: this interplay of scale perceptions is what the designer of this pattern aimed to achieve. The result is printed on light chiffon silk garments from the HI-FICTION SCIENCE collection.

Des spirales chimiques aussi grandes que l'univers ou aussi petites que des molécules au microscope. Ce jeu de perception des grandeurs est l'effet recherché ici, avec une impression sur voile de soie transparent de la collection HI-FICTION SCIENCE (science de haute-fiction).

Chemisch inspirierte Spiralen können so groß wie das Universum oder so klein wie Moleküle unter dem Mikroskop sein. Hier wird mit der Wahrnehmung der Dimensionen gespielt und auf einen durchsichtigen Seidenchiffon der Kollektion HI-FICTION SCIENCE gedruckt.

DARING is part of the DARLING MARLENE collection, inspired by the Art Deco design movement of the 1920s and 30s. This digitally made pattern enhances self-assurance, sensuality and seduction, and has been printed on pure satin.

DARING (osé) fait partie de la collection DARLING MARLENE, inspirée de l'Art déco, un mouvement artistique des années 20 et 30. Le motif, conçu numériquement et imprimé sur du satin pur, renforce l'estime de soi, la sensualité et la séduction.

Auch DARING (Gewagt) aus der Kollektion DARLING MARLENE hat das Art déco, einen Kunststil der 1920er- und 1930er-Jahre, zum Vorbild. Das digital hergestellte Muster setzt auf Selbstsicherheit, Sinnlichkeit und Verführung und wurde auf 100 % Satin gedruckt.

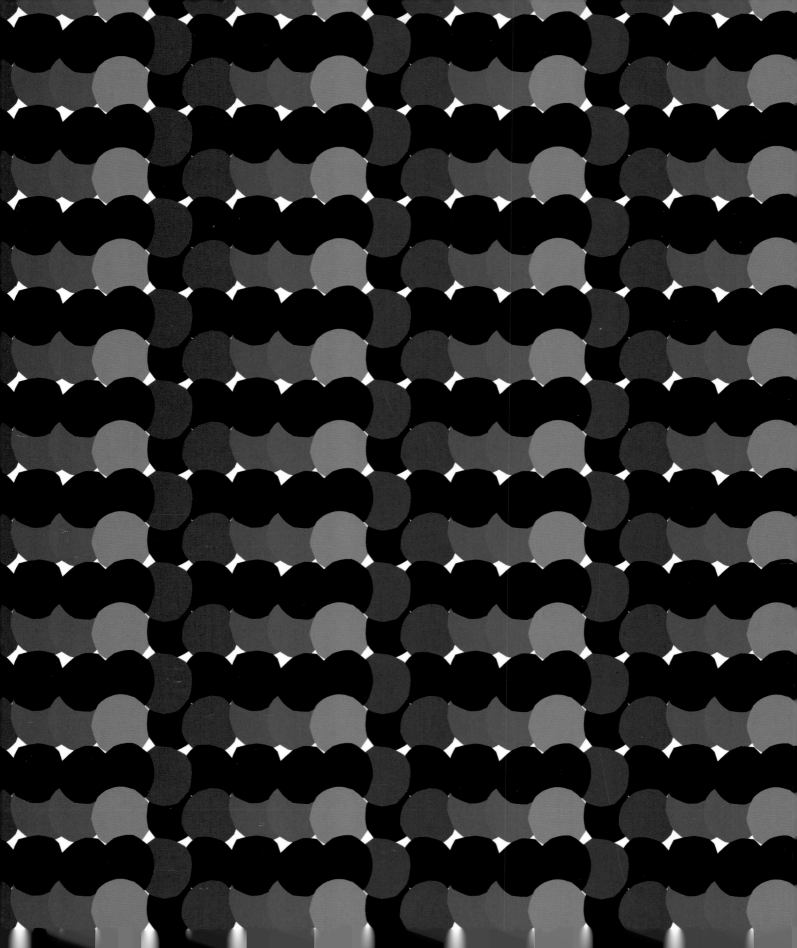

These irregular, circular shapes, placed side by side and colored in various shades of blue, seek to emulate the visual effect of classic checked prints. Perhaps it could be seen as one interpretation of Formula 1 flags. What do you see?

Ces formes circulaires irrégulières, placées les unes à côté des autres et colorées en différents tons bleus, cherchent à imiter l'effet visuel du motif à carreaux classique. Une vision toute personnelle des drapeaux à damier en Formule 1? Interprétez-le à votre guise…

Unregelmäßige Kreisformen sind hier in mehreren Blautönen nebeneinandergesetzt, um den optischen Effekt des klassischen Karodrucks nachzuahmen. Eine persönliche Interpretation der Formel-1-Zielflaggen? Finden Sie Ihre eigene Deutung …

The SNAKES AND LADDERS pattern contains references from the elegant world of sailing: a formal theme that has been rendered in Limedrop's usual playful style.

La collection à laquelle appartient le motif SNAKES AND LADDERS (serpents et échelles) s'inspire du monde élégant de la navigation, un thème, malgré ses apparences sérieuses, que Limedrop a abordé sur le ton ludique qui caractérise son approche de l'esthétique.

Die elegante Kollektion, zu der auch das Muster SNAKES AND LADDERS (Schlangen und Leitern) gehört, hat ihren Ausgangspunkt in der Welt der Nautik. Egal wie ernst das Thema erscheinen mag, hier wird es mit dem typisch verspielten Stil behandelt, mit dem Limedrop die grafische Gestaltung angeht.

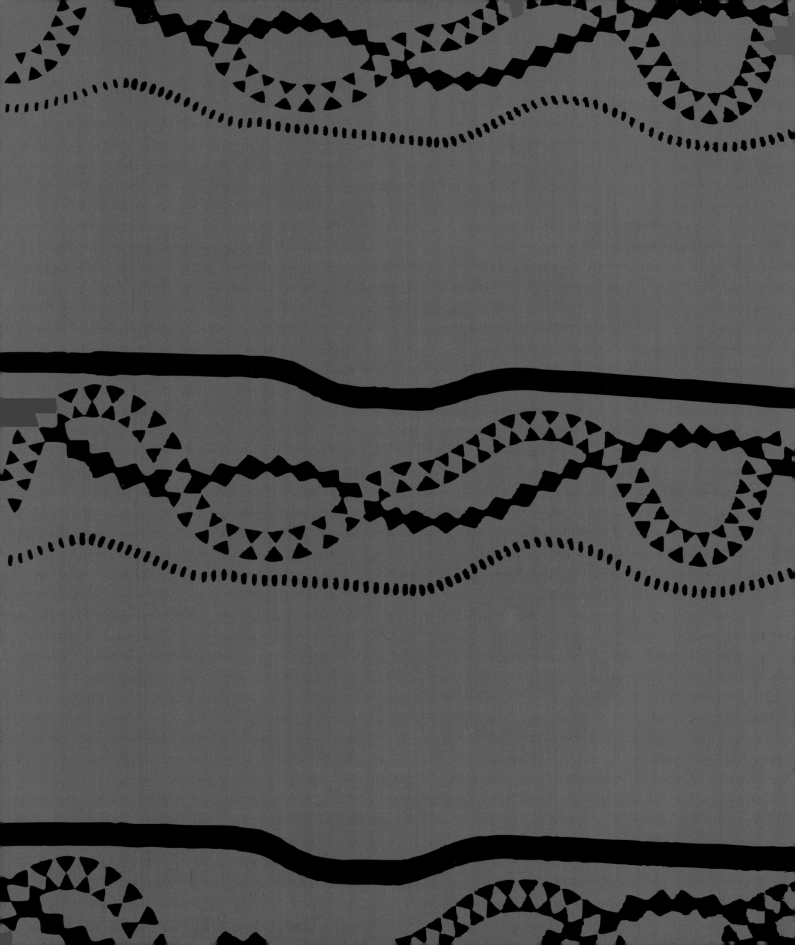

Ostwald Helgason   www.ostwaldhelgason.com

This composition is based on African motifs. Their structure and appearance have been amplified to the point where they have been transformed into new geometrically exaggerated elements. These are presented as ephemeral ideas floating over black-and-white and colored lines.

Les motifs africains sont le thème sous-jacent de cette composition. Sa structure et son aspect ont été développés jusqu'à en faire des éléments nouveaux (exagérément symétriques) qui se présentent comme des idées éphémères flottant sur des rayures noires et blanches.

Dieser Zusammenstellung liegen afrikanische Muster zugrunde. Ihr Aufbau und ihre Optik wurden gedehnt, bis sie sich in neue, übertriebene geometrische Elemente verwandelten, die wie vergängliche Ideen auf schwarzen und weißen Streifen fast schwebend wirken.

This pattern is a new take on the classic Vichy check. The designer decided to use hand-carved rubber stamps to achieve a less rigid effect. This adds texture and a degree of imperfection to the pattern.

Ce motif est une réinterprétation des traditionnels carreaux vichy. Pour obtenir un résultat moins rigide, on a décidé d'utiliser des tampons en liège taillés à la main, qui offrent une texture particulière et une certaine imperfection dans la disposition des différents éléments.

Das Muster interpretiert das klassische Vichykaro neu. Um die Gestaltung zu beleben, entschied man sich für handgeschnittene Gummistempel. Daraus ergab sich eine besondere Textur und eine bewusste Ungenauigkeit bei der Anordnung der Elemente.

Julia Vergara (SuTurno)/Loreak Mendian   www.suturno.net, www.loreakmendian.com

Photo © Jon Uriarte; styling: Nagor Pecharroman; makeup: Ion Sarasola

This pattern was designed as a result of a study of Basque culture—in which many different elements interlink—and traditional Basque dress. The pattern uses hand-carved rubber stamps and plays with the analysis and deconstruction of two crossed lines.

Ce motif est né de l'étude de la culture basque (où convergent des éléments divers et variés) et de ses costumes traditionnels. Il a été réalisé à l'aide de tampons de liège taillés à la main, tout en jouant sur l'analyse et la décomposition de deux lignes croisées.

Seinen Ursprung hat das Muster in der baskischen Kultur mit ihren vielen verschiedenen Elementen und traditionellen Trachten. Für die Ausführung wurden handgeschnittene Gummistempel eingesetzt und man spielte mit der Analyse und Zersetzung von geometrischen Körpern.

Often we become so overwhelmed by daily routines that the only thing we can think of is escaping, slowing down the pace of life, disconnecting, relaxing and unwinding. Just imagine being able to fly north during the summer, like migratory birds.

Combien de fois vous êtes-vous sentis tellement lassés de la routine que vous ne pensiez qu'à vous évader, qu'à freiner un peu le rythme de la vie, déconnecter, vous détendre et vous reposer ? Pouvoir voler sans contraintes vers le Nord pendant l'été comme le font les oiseaux migrateurs…

Wie oft fühlt man sich von Routine erdrückt und denkt nur noch daran, kürzer zu treten und abzuschalten, ans Entspannen und Relaxen? Oder frei und ungebunden wie die Zugvögel im Frühling nach Norden zu ziehen …

Inspired by construction materials and toy trucks—as a way of connecting with our inner child—this pattern combines truck motifs with organic shapes, playing with solids, voids and color.

Inspiré des engins de construction et des camions miniatures (une manière de retrouver l'enfant qui sommeille en nous), ce motif allie des contours de camions et des éléments organiques, qui jonglent à la perfection avec les espaces pleins, vides, et l'application des couleurs.

Baumaterial und Spielzeuglaster bilden die Grundlage für dieses Muster und wecken das Kind, das in uns allen steckt. Hier verbinden sich die Konturen von Lastern und organischen Motiven in einem strategischen Spiel mit Fülle, Lücken und Farbe.

This pattern is based on the kingfisher: the mythical bird of Greek legend that mysteriously calms the winds and waves when it nests on the sea. Here, the flock rises from a colorful mass, becoming increasingly easier to discern before dispersing in the black.

Motif inspiré du martin-pêcheur, un oiseau de la mythologie grecque, dont on raconte que, lorsqu'il nichait en mer, les vents et les vagues s'apaisaient mystérieusement. Ici, la volée s'élève depuis une masse colorée, devenant de plus en plus nette jusqu'à se fondre dans le noir.

Das Muster basiert auf dem mystischen Eisvogel der griechischen Legende, der Wind und Wellen auf geheimnisvolle Weise beruhigt haben soll, um auf dem Meer nisten zu können. Hier erhebt sich der Schwarm aus einer farbigen Masse und wird immer deutlicher, um sich dann in der Schwärze zu verlieren.

Movement is crucial in this pattern, which has been named TURBULENCE. It illustrates flocks of birds flying in the air and seen from a distance. The birds blend into the wind and the waves of the sea during a tempestuous winter.

Le mouvement est l'élément clé de ce motif appelé TURBULENCE (turbulence) et qui évoque des nuées d'oiseaux s'élevant dans les airs, observées à très longue distance. Elles se mélangent et se confondent avec le vent et la houle pendant une saison hivernale agitée.

Das Kernmotiv des Musters nennt sich TURBULENCE (Turbulenz) und besteht aus fliegenden Vogelschwärmen, die aus weiter Ferne betrachtet werden. Sie vermengen sich während eines turbulenten Wintersturms mit dem Wind und den Meereswogen.

The key to this pattern is the decontextualization of its elements. The seemingly hand-drawn geometric African motifs lose their ethnicity, however, due to the modern color combination used: cyan with black.

L'originalité de ce motif réside dans la décontextualisation de ses éléments. Les motifs géométriques africains, qui semblent avoir été tracés à main levée, perdent de leur valeur ethnique par l'application d'une combinaison de couleurs moderne telle que le cyan et le noir.

Der Schlüssel zu diesem Muster liegt darin, dass die Elemente außerhalb ihres Kontexts zitiert werden. Afrikanisch-geometrische Motive, die mit freier Hand gezeichnet scheinen, verlieren ihren ethnischen Gehalt durch moderne Farbkombinationen wie Cyan mit Schwarz.

The seabed is shrouded in mystery. There, you can find the rare plants, exotic corals, underwater caves and terrifying fish that have provided inspiration for stories, films—and this pattern.

Le fond des mers est un monde rempli de secrets. On peut y trouver des plantes curieuses, des coraux exotiques, des grottes sous-marines ou d'affreux poissons qui font frémir – une grande variété qui a inspiré de nombreux contes, films et ce motif.

Die Welt am Meeresgrund steckt voller Geheimnisse. Dort finden sich eigenartige Pflanzen, Korallen, unterirdische Höhlen und Furcht erregende Fische. So vielfältig ist diese Welt, dass sie Geschichten, Filme und auch dieses Muster inspiriert hat.

This pattern of small, rounded shapes transports us to a leafy world that could easily be interpreted as a forest full of mushrooms, a magic forest with strange little leaves or a lush forest of golf clubs. And why not?

Ce motif réalisé à partir de petites figures arrondies nous plonge dans un monde dense qui pourrait très bien être perçu comme un bois rempli de champignons, une forêt enchantée avec de minuscules et étranges feuilles ou, pourquoi pas, une jungle luxuriante de clubs de golf.

Das Muster aus kleinen Figuren mit gerundeten Köpfen versetzt uns in eine Welt, die leicht als Wald voller Pilze, verzauberter Urwald mit winzigen, eigenartigen Blättern oder auch – warum nicht? – als dichter Forst aus Golfschlägern interpretiert werden kann.

ILLUSIONIST is based on a fragmented star in a multidimensional space that is reminiscent of the classic shapes of Q*bert—an 80s arcade game. The design uses different colors to offset its various levels.

Le point de départ du motif ILLUSIONIST (illusionniste) est une étoile décomposée sur les côtés fractionnés d'un espace multidimensionnel qui rappellent les formes du jeu d'arcade typique des années 80, Q*bert. Les couleurs servent à distinguer les différents plans.

Die Grundlage von ILLUSIONIST bildet ein Stern, der in einem multidimensionalen Raum in Einzelteile zerlegt wurde. Diese wiederum erinnern an das klassische Arcadespiel „Q*bert" aus den 1980er-Jahren. Zur Unterscheidung der einzelnen Ebenen wird Farbe eingesetzt.

This geometric pattern, called DIAMOND SCALES, depicts fish scales. The hints of color have been arranged in a slightly irregular fashion, lending the pattern a close affinity with nature.

Ce motif géométrique appelé DIAMOND SCALES (écailles de diamant) représente les écailles d'un poisson qui évolue en haute mer. Les touches de couleur ont été réparties de manière aléatoire, ce qui nous rapproche de la spontanéité de la nature.

Das geometrische Muster DIAMOND SCALES (Diamantschuppen) ist den Schuppen von Hochseefischen nachempfunden. Die Farbakzente sind in einem leicht unregelmäßigen Rhythmus gesetzt, sodass sie spontan und natürlich wirken.

With the aim of supporting urban projects for the extension and improvement of bike lanes, this pattern includes all manner of bicycles: big ones, ones with baskets, ones with one big and one small wheel, tandems, road bikes, mountain bikes and classic Dutch bicycles.

De grands vélos, avec des paniers, une grande et une petite roue, des tandems, des vélos de course, de montagne, les bicyclettes hollandaises… tous les modèles de vélos ont leur place sur ce motif qui vise à soutenir le développement et l'amélioration des pistes cyclables dans les villes.

Große Fahrräder, Fahrräder mit Körben, mit einem großen und einem kleinen Rad, Tandems, Rennräder, Mountainbikes und klassische Hollandräder – alle tauchen sie in diesem Muster auf, das für Ausbau und Verbesserung von städtischen Fahrradwegen wirbt.

The exotic, tropical collection of which this pattern is part was inspired by the designer's accidental discovery of a remote desert island in the Pacific called Potipot, while surfing the Web, and by a trip to Costa Rica. The design evokes bamboo, palm trees and Aboriginal huts.

La découverte fortuite sur Internet de Potipot, une île perdue dans le Pacifique, et un voyage au Costa Rica sont les sources d'inspiration de cette collection exotique et tropicale dont fait partie ce motif qui rappelle le bambou, les palmiers et les cabanes des aborigènes.

Eine Reise nach Costa Rica und die einsame Pazifikinsel Potipot – eine zufällige Entdeckung beim Surfen im Internet – dienten als Anregung für die exotische Kollektion, zu der auch dieses Muster mit Reminiszenzen an Bambus, Palmen und tropische Urwaldhütten gehört.

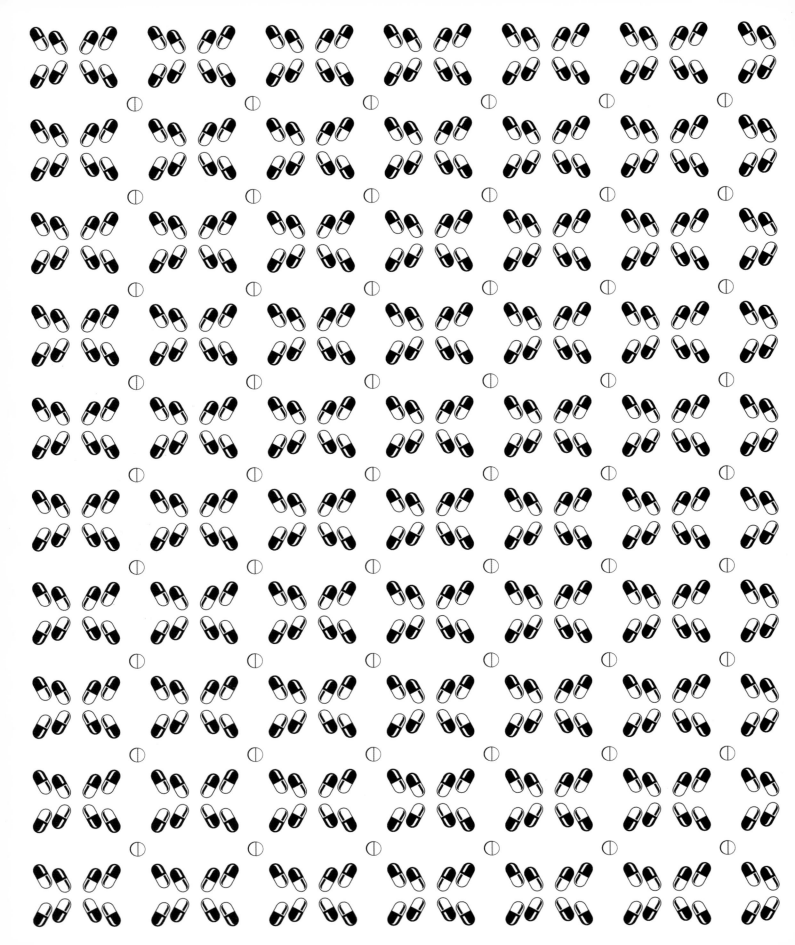

This pattern is part of a collection that transports us back to that difficult period in our lives when we thought our time was up and that there was no way out. PILLS & TABLETS resembles a Victorian-style pattern, but it is actually made up of mini tranquilizers and pills.

Ce motif fait partie d'une collection qui nous rappelle ces moments difficiles où l'on croit être mort et où l'on sent qu'il n'y a aucune échappatoire. PILLS & TABLETS (pilules et comprimés) ressemble à un imprimé victorien réalisé à partir d'anxiolytiques et de cachets.

Das Muster dieser Kollektion versetzt den Betrachter in jene schwierigen Momente, in denen man wünschte, man wäre tot und aus dem es kein Entkommen zu geben scheint. PILLS & TABLETS erinnert an viktorianische Drucke, zeigt aber Pillen und Tabletten.

Tiny flowers joined by fine lines of branches group and scatter like small continents blown by the wind, engendering movement and changing light effects that give rise to different shades of green. The design blends classic oriental wallpaper with modern camouflage patterns.

De minuscules fleurs reliées par de fins traits d'écorce se regroupent et se dispersent tels de petits continents au fil du vent, dont le mouvement et le changement de lumière créent des nuances de vert. Un mélange de tapisserie orientale classique et imprimé moderne de camouflage.

Winzige Blätter an feinen Zweigen werden vom Wind bewegt. Der Windhauch und das Spiel von Licht und Schatten entstehen durch unterschiedliche Grünnuancen. Eine Kombination aus klassischen orientalischen Teppichmustern und modernem Tarndruck.

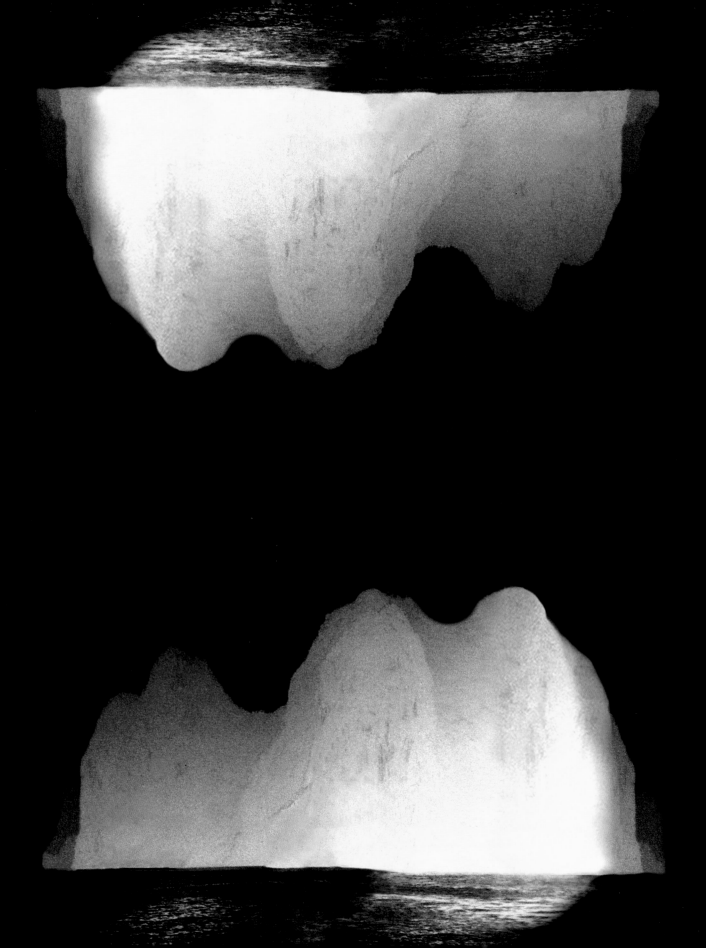

© Olivia Hemus

This pattern is based on a sinister black body of water with moonlit limestone cliffs emerging from its depths. Printed onto a shiny shift, these reflections swirl with volume and silently creep into the garment from the hem, forming astonishing shapes.

De sinistres eaux noires reflètent des falaises calcaires émergeant des profondeurs éclairées par la clarté de la lune. Des reflets sur une large robe brillante qui tourbillonnent avec le volume et apparaissent discrètement dans l'ourlet, telles des formes effrayantes.

Im unheimlichen schwarzen Wasser spiegeln sich Kalksteinklippen, die aus mondbeschienenen Meerestiefen aufragen. Die Spiegelungen auf dem weiten, glänzenden Kleid werden durch das Körpervolumen verwirbelt und steigen als schimmernde Formen vom Saum auf.

The components of this themed, natural-colored pattern are branches of trees drawn with watered-down India ink and arranged such that they recall upright spikes. For winter 2007, this pattern was printed onto heavy fabric destined to make coats and suits.

Ce motif, au thème et coloris végétal, est composé de branches d'arbres dessinées à l'encre de Chine diluée et disposées de telle sorte qu'elles suggèrent la forme d'un épi. En hiver 2007, il a été imprimé sur des tissus épais pour confectionner des manteaux et des costumes.

Mit wässriger Tusche gezeichnete Blätter sind so angeordnet, dass sie Halme bilden und sich zu einem Pflanzenmuster zusammenschließen. Im Winter 2007 wurde es auf dicke Stoffe gedruckt, um Mäntel und Kostüme zu zieren.

MULTICOLORED
MULTICOLORE
BUNT

Nando & Silvia (potipoti) www.potipoti.com

The elements featuring in this composition are pieces of a vintage wooden game resembling old, multicolored totem poles typical of the indigenous peoples of Canada and Alaska. The pattern is a fusion of fables, folklore and fun.

Les éléments utilisés pour créer cette composition sont des pièces en bois d'un jeu vintage qui rappellent les anciens totems en bois taillé et polychromé, typiques des peuples indigènes du Canada et de l'Alaska. Un mélange entre fable, folklore et fantaisie.

Die für diese Zusammenstellung verwendeten Elemente gehören zu einem antiken Holzspiel. Sie erinnern an alte Totems aus geschnitztem, mehrfarbigem Holz, die für Stammeskunst aus Kanada und Alaska typisch sind. So gehen Fabeln, Folklore und Spiel eine Verbindung ein.

© Marc Debnam

The colors of the poppy, the Cadillacs and the loungers by the pool in the movie *The Flamingo Kid* and the bronzed bodies of kitsch beach culture lend shape to this pattern, which shows beautiful girls in bikinis with their suitors, soaking up the sun to the max.

Les couleurs du coquelicot, les Cadillac, les transats au bord de la piscine du film *The Flamingo Kid* et les corps bronzés de la culture kitsch de la plage composent ce motif qui montre de belles filles en bikini, accompagnées de leurs prétendants et en train de se dorer au soleil.

Klatschmohnfarben, Cadillacs, Poolliegen aus dem Film *Flamingo Kid* und sonnengebräunte Körper – mit einem Muster aus attraktiven Bikiniträgerinnen und ihren Verehrern fängt dieses Beachmuster die Sonne ein.

STR
STRING REPUBLIC

When drawing SWEET MAKES ME SWEET, its creator envisaged and was inspired by girls who like, and delight in, treating themselves with candy, ice cream, chocolate and all things sweet. The pattern is also a tribute to the girls who have made him just as happy.

En dessinant SWEET MAKES ME SWEET (le sucré me rend sucré), son créateur a imaginé, et s'en est inspiré, des jeunes filles qui aiment les sucreries, les glaces, le chocolat et toutes sortes de sucreries. De plus, ce motif est un petit hommage aux jeunes filles qui le rendent heureux.

Als der Designer SWEET MAKES ME SWEET (Süßes macht mich süß) entwarf, dachte er an Mädchen, die Süßigkeiten, Eis, Schokolade und alles, was süß ist, mögen. Außerdem ist das Muster eine kleine Hommage an die Mädchen, die ihn glücklich machen.

The decorative elements of the 50s, and the birds and the gardens of the ladies of that era, were the inspiration for this *toile de Jouy*, in which bunches of bubble-gum pink carnations float above a textured collage of golden feathers.

Les ornements féminins des années 50, ainsi que les oiseaux et les jardins des dames de cette époque, ont inspiré cette Toile de Jouy où des bouquets d'œillets couleur chewing-gum reposent sans contrainte sur un collage texturé de plumes dorées.

Modeaccessoires der 1950er-Jahre sowie Vögel und Gärten jener Zeit dienten als Anregung für diese Toile-de-Jouy. Sie kombiniert Nelken in Kaugummifarben mühelos mit einer Struktur-collage aus vergoldeten Federn.

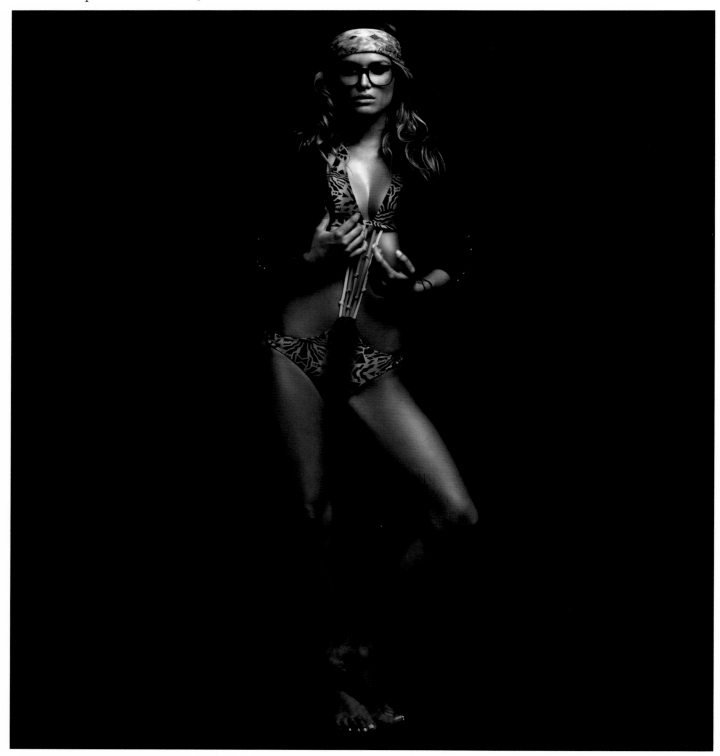

Africa and its tribal sculptures and exotic animals were the initial inspiration for this pattern, which follows the premise that, to be truly original, designs should always be based on organic or natural elements. In this case, it really works.

L' Afrique, ses sculptures tribales et ses animaux ont initialement inspiré ce motif basé sur le postulat que l'imprimé doit toujours provenir d'un élément organique ou être en rapport avec la nature pour garantir son originalité. Ici, cela a fonctionné à la perfection.

Afrikanische Stammesskulpturen und Tiere waren ursprünglich Inspiration für dieses Muster. Es folgt dem Gedanken, dass ein originelles Design stets auch etwas Organisches haben oder Natur-elemente aufweisen sollte. In diesem Fall ist dies auch gelungen.

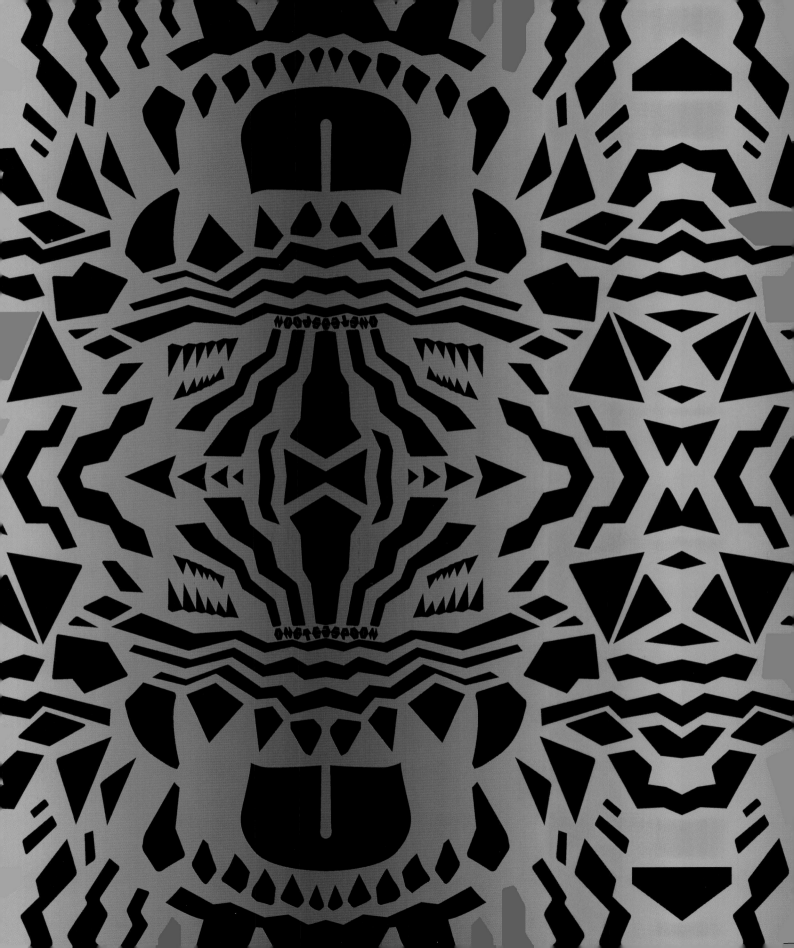

© Six 6 Photography

Seen from afar, the miniature tools in this colorful grid create a visual effect of electric impulses. This structured, shiny satin dress with geometric neckline was inspired by mathematical and geometric equations.

Vus de loin, les outils miniatures de ce quadrillage coloré font penser à des pulsations électriques. Cette robe structurée au décolleté géométrique (confectionnée en satin brillant) s'inspire des équations mathématiques et géométriques.

Von Weitem wirken die bunten Miniaturwerkzeuge des Rasters wie die optische Darstellung elektrischer Impulse. Das Kleid aus strukturiertem glänzendem Satinstoff hat einen geometrischen Ausschnitt und nimmt sich mathematische und geometrische Gleichungen zum Vorbild.

This pattern—which at first sight is reminiscent of waves at high tide—captures the true inspiration of Art Deco and of old theaters, resembling the dome of the Chrysler Building in New York or the boxes of the Teatro La Scala in Milan.

Ces ondes, qui à première vue rappellent les vagues sur la mer à marée haute, tirent leur véritable inspiration de l'Art déco et des anciens théâtres, et peuvent donc être comparées à la coupole du bâtiment Chrysler de New York ou aux loges de La Scala de Milan.

Die Wellen, die auf den ersten Blick an Meereswogen bei Flut erinnern, sind in Wirklichkeit vom Art déco und alten Theaterbauten angeregt. Sie lassen an die Bogenformen des Chrysler Building in New York oder die Logen der Mailänder Scala denken.

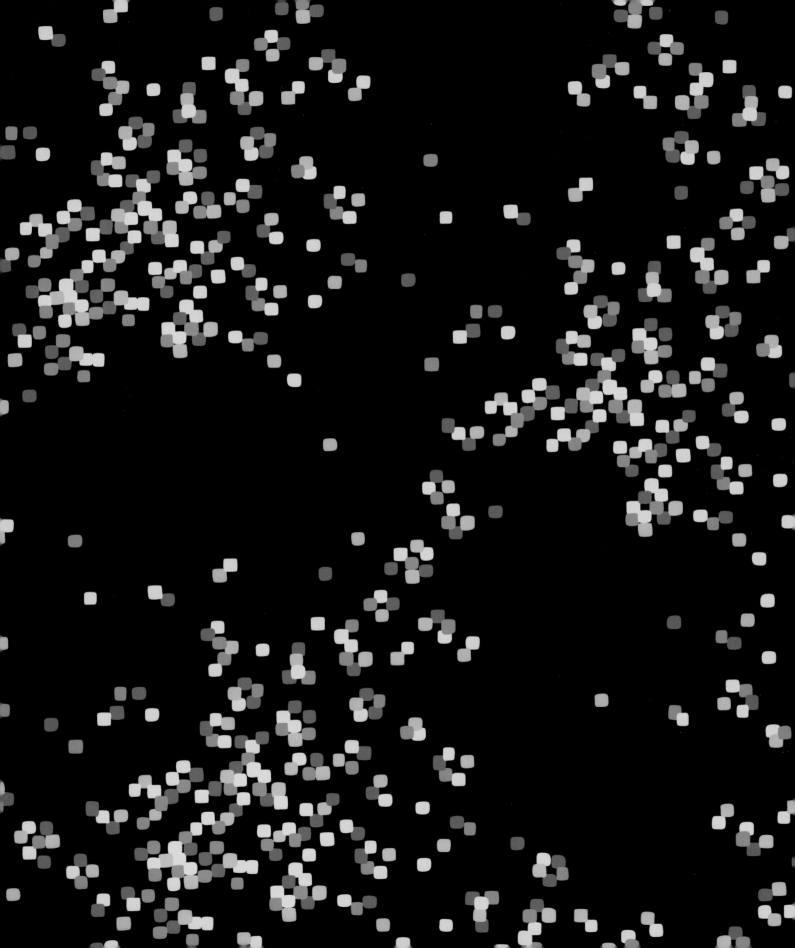

It is one of those days when the sun shines high in the sky, the temperature is perfect for a stroll along the waterfront and you are just happy to take in the scent of the ocean and the sound of the gulls. Days like these make you want to fill the sky with colorful confetti.

Une de ces journées où le soleil brille au zénith, la température est idéale pour se promener sur le rivage et profiter simplement de l'odeur de la mer et du cri des mouettes. Une de ces journées où l'on a envie de remplir le ciel de confettis colorés.

Ein Tag mit strahlendem Sonnenschein, idealen Temperaturen für einen Spaziergang über die Strandpromenade, salzigem Meeresgeruch und dem Geschrei der Möwen. An solch glücklichen Tagen möchte man buntes Konfetti in die Luft werfen.

The marine aesthetics of caravels, the elegance and mystery of the night, and of storms and the sea, heavy clouds, dark skies, stars, roses, bows, patched sails, anchors and kingfishers. These elements all play a part in this romantic, mysterious dream.

L'esthétique marine des caravelles, l'élégance et le mystère de la nuit et des tempêtes en mer. Nuages sombres, ciels couverts, étoiles, roses, rubans, voiles en coupons, ancres et martins-pêcheurs sont les principaux éléments de ce rêve romantique et mystérieux.

Karavellenästhetik, Eleganz und Geheimnis der Nacht, Sturm auf dem Meer. Dräuende Wolken, düsterer Himmel, Sterne, Rosen, Schleifen, Segel aus Stoffresten, Anker und Eisvögel: Sie alle sind Hauptdarsteller in diesem romantischen und geheimnisvollen Traum.

It is a gray fall day, the sun is hidden from sight and it is about to rain. Today seems like a perfect day to sit in front of a fire and venture out only if it rains colorful drops, like those in this pattern, which fall to cheer and brighten fall fashion.

Un jour gris d'automne, où le soleil ne veut pas poindre et que la pluie est imminente, invite à rester chez soi près de la cheminée et à ne pas sortir du tout, sauf si la pluie est formée de gouttes colorées qui tombent du ciel en égayant et en éclairant la mode automnale.

Ein grauer Herbsttag ohne Sonnenstrahlen, an dem es jeden Moment zu regnen anfängt, ist ideal, um es sich zuhause gemütlich zu machen und nicht vor die Tür zu gehen – außer wenn bunte Tropfen vom Himmel fallen und die Herbstmode bunt und fröhlich machen.

BIG FLOWERS NIGHT is inspired by dreams, the romance of the night, and both terrestrial and marine flora. Butterflies, flowers, birds and algae play, mix and merge in this colorful, dreamlike landscape that is both mysterious and elegant.

BIG FLOWERS NIGHT (nuit des grandes fleurs) s'inspire des rêves, du romantisme de la nuit et de la flore tant marine que terrestre. Papillons, fleurs, algues et oiseaux jouent, se mêlent et se confondent dans ce paysage onirique aux coloris mystérieux et élégants.

BIG FLOWERS NIGHT (Nacht großer Blumen) wurde von Träumen, romantischen Nächten und der Flora im Meer und zu Lande inspiriert. Schmetterlinge, Blumen, Algen und Vögel kommen spielerisch zusammen und verlieren sich in einer geheimnisvollen Traumlandschaft, die mit eleganten Farben gestaltet wurde.

Animal prints are very popular in the fashion world, and this is no exception. This pattern's originality lies in it being based on the unique and exotic shell of a turtle, whose surface is simulated with strong, saturated colors.

Les animaux sont un motif très fréquent dans le monde de la mode. Ce cas ne fait pas exception ; son originalité réside dans le choix d'une base atypique et exotique pour le motif : il s'agit d'une carapace de tortue dont les couches ont été colorées dans des tons vifs et saturés.

Tiermotive finden sich häufig in der Modewelt. Dieses exotische Muster ist keine Ausnahme: Originell ist hier, dass es auf einem Schildkröten-panzer beruht, dessen Musterung mit kräftigen satten Farben angedeutet wird.

Manuela Helg, Karin Maurer (Beige)   www.beige.ch

Irregularity prevails in this pattern, which is a jumble of barcodes, sticks from the classic game of Mikado and rainforest motifs. The design combines the concept of watermarking with stripes that move randomly through oscillating layers of abstract forms.

L'irrégularité est la loi qui régit ce motif ressemblant à une fusion chaotique entre codes-barres, baguettes du fameux jeu Mikado et forêt tropicale. Il mêle le concept de filigrane avec des rayures qui se déplacent au hasard sur des couches oscillantes aux formes abstraites.

Unregelmäßigkeit ist das Hauptcharakteristikum dieses Musters, das wie eine chaotische Kombination aus Strichcodes, Mikadostäben und tropischem Urwald anmutet. Die filigrane Gestaltung wird durch Streifen erreicht, die sich aufs Gerate-wohl durch bewegte abstrakte Formen ziehen.

This creation was directly inspired by the Muslim mosaic heritage. The pattern uses the typical mosaic interplay and intersection of straight lines to create the illusion of perfect circles, which are highlighted with strong colors, such as red and bottle green.

L'héritage musulman que constituent les mosaïques sert de source d'inspiration directe à cette composition. Comme sur les motifs originaux, le jeu du croisement des lignes droites crée l'illusion de cercles parfaits, mis en valeur par des couleurs vives telles que le vert foncé ou le rouge.

Das moslemische Erbe der Mosaiken diente dieser Zusammenstellung als unmittelbare Anregung. Wie bei den Originalen erwecken Spiel und Schnittstellen gerader Linien den Eindruck perfekter Kreise, die durch kräftige Farben wie Dunkelgrün und Rot hervorgehoben werden.

This pattern is based on a sporting style, with lines of different colors and thicknesses intersecting at varying intervals. This causes the fabric—a soft Chinese silk crepe—to look gradated and—when seen from afar—as if it has different textures.

Ce motif obéit à un graphisme sportif, avec des lignes de différentes couleurs et épaisseurs qui s'entrecroisent de manière irrégulière. De loin, cette composition donne au tissu (un crêpe très doux en soie chinoise) un aspect dégradé de différentes textures.

Das Muster orientiert sich an der Sportgrafik, indem es Linien unterschiedlicher Farben und Stärken in wechselndem Rhythmus kreuzt. Daher erweckt der Stoff, ein zarter chinesischer Seidenkrepp, von Weitem den Eindruck unterschiedlicher Texturen.

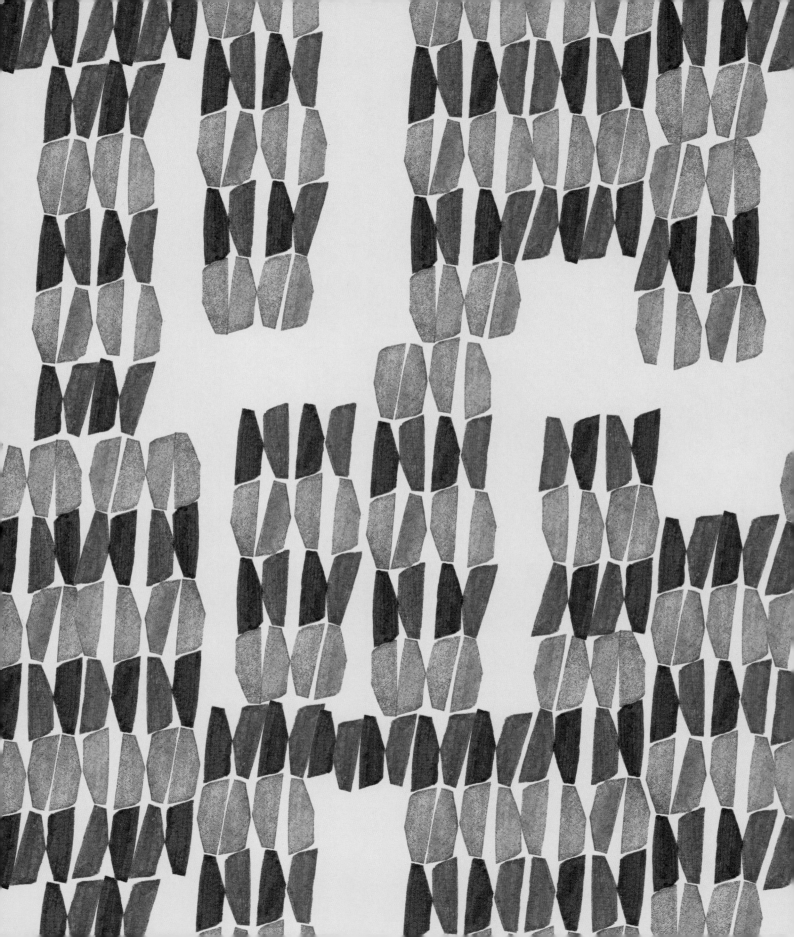

ROCAS (rocks) is based on the repetition of several irregular forms that try to fit into each other. These blocks of color are created using handcrafted rubber stamps, forming a randomly arranged pattern that suggests texture and movement.

ROCAS (roches) est basé sur la répétition de formes irrégulières cherchant à s'emboîter. Ces modules sont faits à la main avec des tampons en liège, une technique qui donne une certaine texture alors que la disposition désordonnée des pièces crée un léger mouvement.

ROCAS (Felsen) basiert auf der Wiederholung mehrerer unregelmäßiger Formen, die aufeinander abgestimmt sind. Module aus handgefertigten Gummistempeln sorgen für eine gewisse Textur, während die ungenaue Anordnung der Elemente dynamisch wirkt.

In this version of the classic leopard print, the creator decided to play with colors, to use a smaller print that is easier to wear—as it is less flashy—and to create a mosaic effect by sharpening the curves of the pattern and placing the elements close together.

Cette réinterprétation du motif léopard classique se distingue néanmoins par ses jeux de couleurs, l'utilisation de formes de petite taille (moins voyant donc plus facile à porter) et la création d'un effet mosaïque en accentuant les courbes et en les disposant côte à côte.

Bei dieser Neuinterpretation des klassischen Leopardendrucks entschied man sich für das Spiel mit Farben und eine kleinteilige, mosaikartige Musterung – sie ist weniger auffällig und damit tragbarer. Die Konturen wurden geschärft und sehr eng aneinandergesetzt.

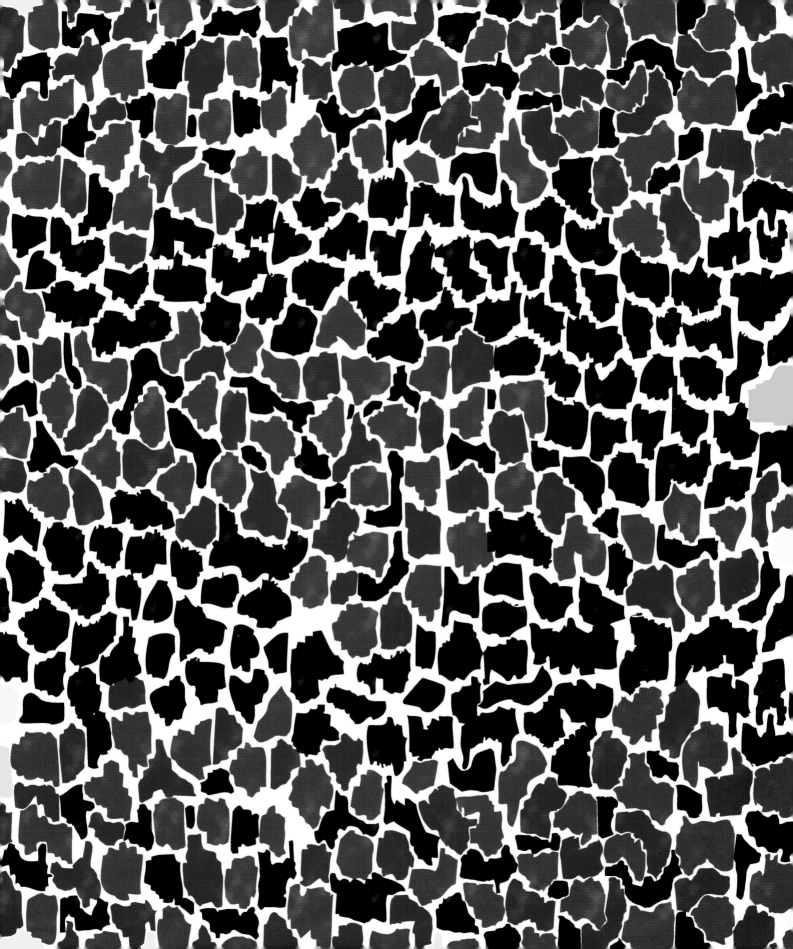

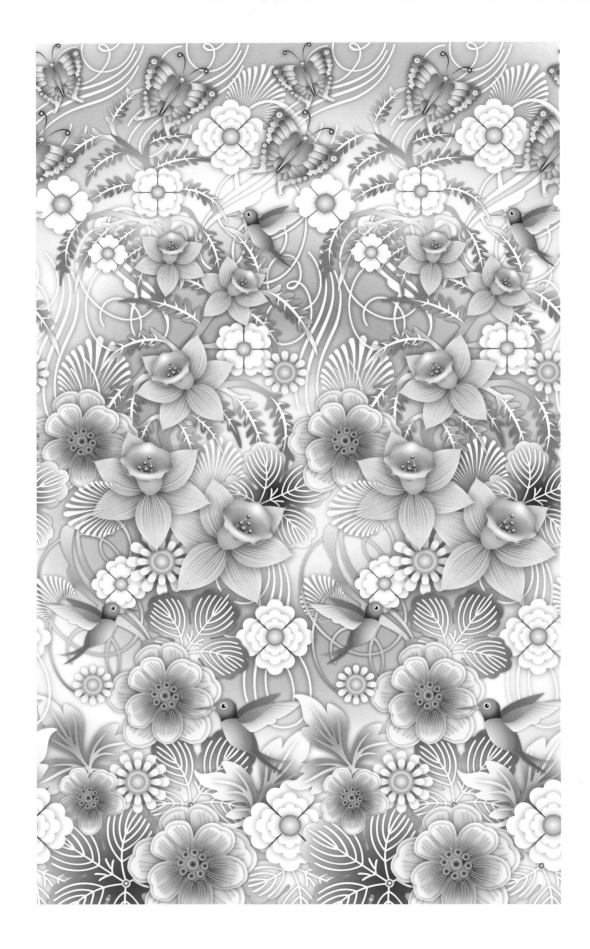